TAYLOR SWIFT

A Life In Pictures

Carolyn McHugh

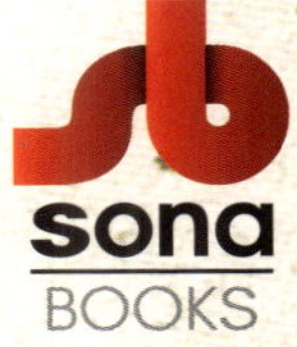

sona
BOOKS

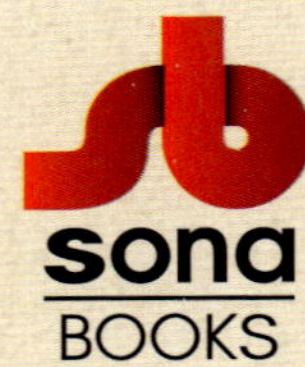

sona BOOKS

Photography courtesy of

Getty images:

- Kevin Mazur
- Dave Hoga
- Rob Verhorst/Redferns
- Sandra Mu
- Christopher Polk/Billboards2012
- Christopher Polk/TAS
- Kevork Djansezian
- Dimitrios Kambouris/LP5
- Sascha Schuermann
- John Medina
- Kevin Winter
- John Medina
- Valerie Macon/AFP
- Jun Sato/GC Images
- Ethan Miller
- Jeff Kravitz/FilmMagic
- Michael Buckner
- Emma McIntyre/AMA2019
- Rick Diamond/WireImage
- TAS Rights Management 2020
- Rich Fury
- Robert Gauthier/Los Angeles Times
- Taylor Hill/FilmMagic

- John Shearer/AMA2019
- Attitude Magazine
- Alliance for Women in Media Foundation
- ANGELA WEISS/AFP
- Raymond Hall/GC
- Mark Metcalfe/TAS
- Andreas Rentz
- Jason Squires/WireImage
- Christopher Polk/ACMA2012
- Matt Winkelmeyer/TAS18
- Rich Fury for iHeartMedia
- Zhang Hengwei/China News Service/VCG
- Dimitrios Kambouris
- Amy Sussman
- John Shearer/TAS23
- Bob Levey/TAS23
- Scott Eisen/TAS23
- Hector Vivas/TAS23
- Buda Mendes/TAS23
- Graham Denholm/TAS24
- Ashok Kumar/TAS24
- Rodin Eckenroth

Alamy images:

- WENN Rights Ltd
- Album
- Everett Collection Inc
- Sharon Dobson
- Associated Press
- BFA
- PA Images

Other images Wiki Commons

Book layout & design Darren Grice at Ctrl-d
Additional writing and editing: Emilie Murray.
Proof reader Cameron Thurlow.

Made in UAE.
ISBN: 978-1-915343-67-3

CONTENTS

INTRO

Taylor Swift, the superstar American singer-songwriter, stands as one of the biggest and best-selling music artists in the world. Since bursting onto the scene as a 16-year-old country sensation in 2006, Taylor has remained a prolific force in the industry, consistently delivering chart-topping hits that resonate with audiences worldwide.

Now in her thirties, Taylor shows no signs of slowing down. With record sales surpassing 200 million worldwide and the title of the most streamed female artist on Spotify, she continues to solidify her status as a musical powerhouse. Her newest album The Tortured Poets Department, released on April 19th 2024 shattered records with an astounding 300 million streams in its first 24 hours, further cementing her place in music history.

But Taylor's influence extends far beyond the recording studio. With her exceptional talent, shrewd business acumen, and unwavering courage, she is settled among that rarified group of artists, including Michael Jackson and Madonna, capable of combining critical acclaim with commercial success.

Evolving beyond her status as a chart-topping mainstream artist, she emerges as a formidable entrepreneur, a committed philanthropist, and a bold champion for progress.

She has headlined six global concert tours, including her latest endeavour, the colossal Eras tour. This ambitious three-hour-plus spectacle features a 44-song set split into 10 acts, each celebrating one of her albums. Universally acclaimed by critics and audiences alike, Taylor's performances showcase her remarkable vocals and musicianship, captivating audiences with her unparalleled talent and stage presence.

This is a look back at Taylor Swift's extraordinary journey through the eras.

DEBUT ERA 2006

A Star is Born

Taylor Swift seemed destined for stardom from the very start. When Scott and Andrea, two successful financiers, gave birth to their first child, Taylor Alison Swift on December 13th, 1989, they decided to name her after their favourite singer James Taylor. Originally, they thought that a gender-neutral name would serve her well for a career in business. That name proved to be a fortunate choice – although not in the way her parents had originally imagined. Did they perhaps have a sense she would grow up to be a superstar?

Taylor spent the first years of her life on the idyllic-sounding, 11-acre, Christmas Tree Farm in West Reading, Pennsylvania in the north-east of America, growing up with her younger brother Austin. As a young girl, Taylor had the run of the place and revelled in the space and nature of those woodlands, crediting her time there with helping to stoke her vivid imagination and creativity.'

While her parents have always been, and remain, a guiding force in her life, it was her maternal grandmother Marjorie Finlay that first sparked her passion for music. Marjorie was a professional opera singer and had a flair for performance, a trait her granddaughter surely inherited.

Taylor often felt 'different' from her peers, her love of country music was unusual for a girl of her age. Taylor became a fan of country when she was just six and first heard music from teenage country star LeAnn Rimes.

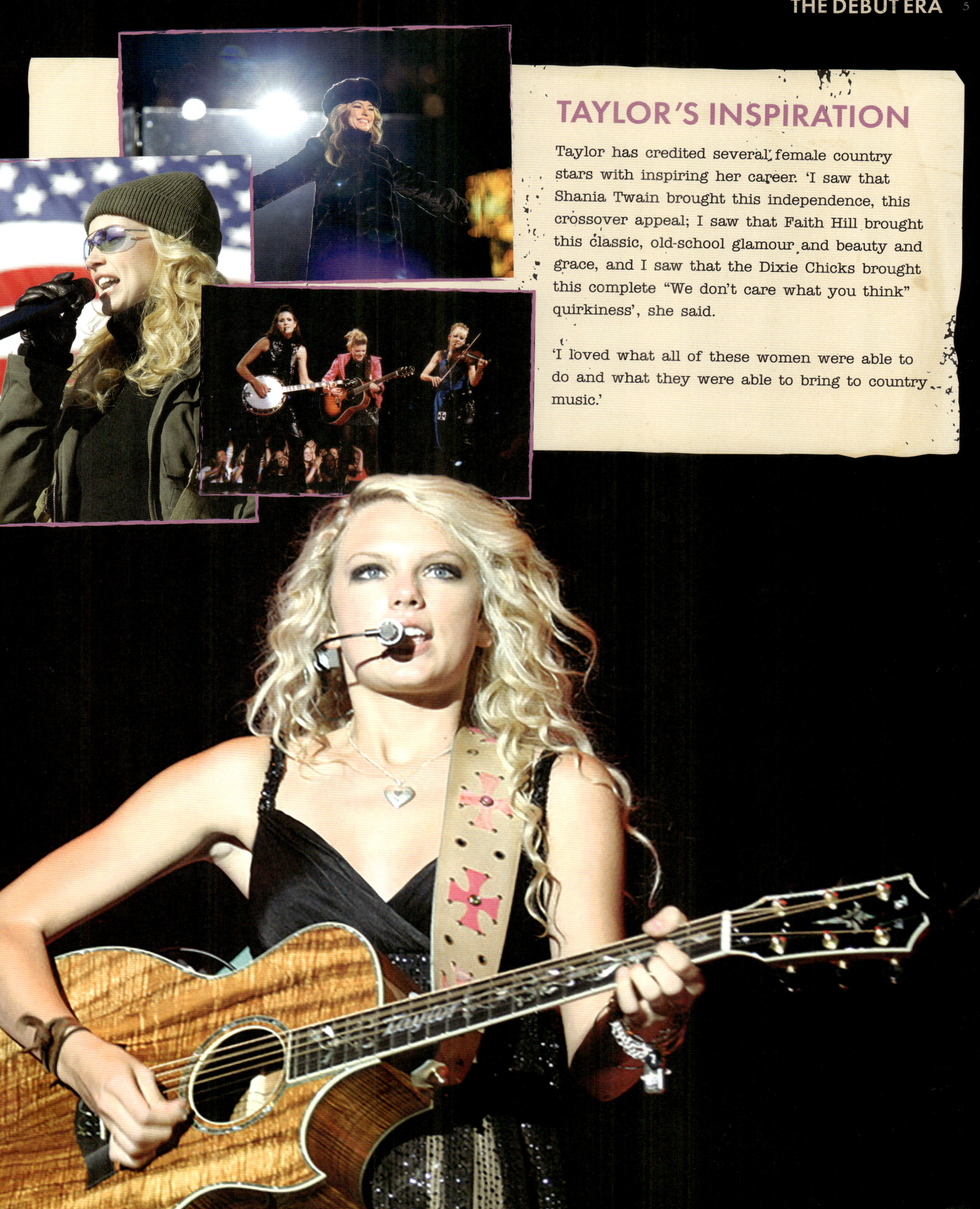

TAYLOR'S INSPIRATION

Taylor has credited several female country stars with inspiring her career. 'I saw that Shania Twain brought this independence, this crossover appeal; I saw that Faith Hill brought this classic, old-school glamour and beauty and grace, and I saw that the Dixie Chicks brought this complete "We don't care what you think" quirkiness', she said.

'I loved what all of these women were able to do and what they were able to bring to country music.'

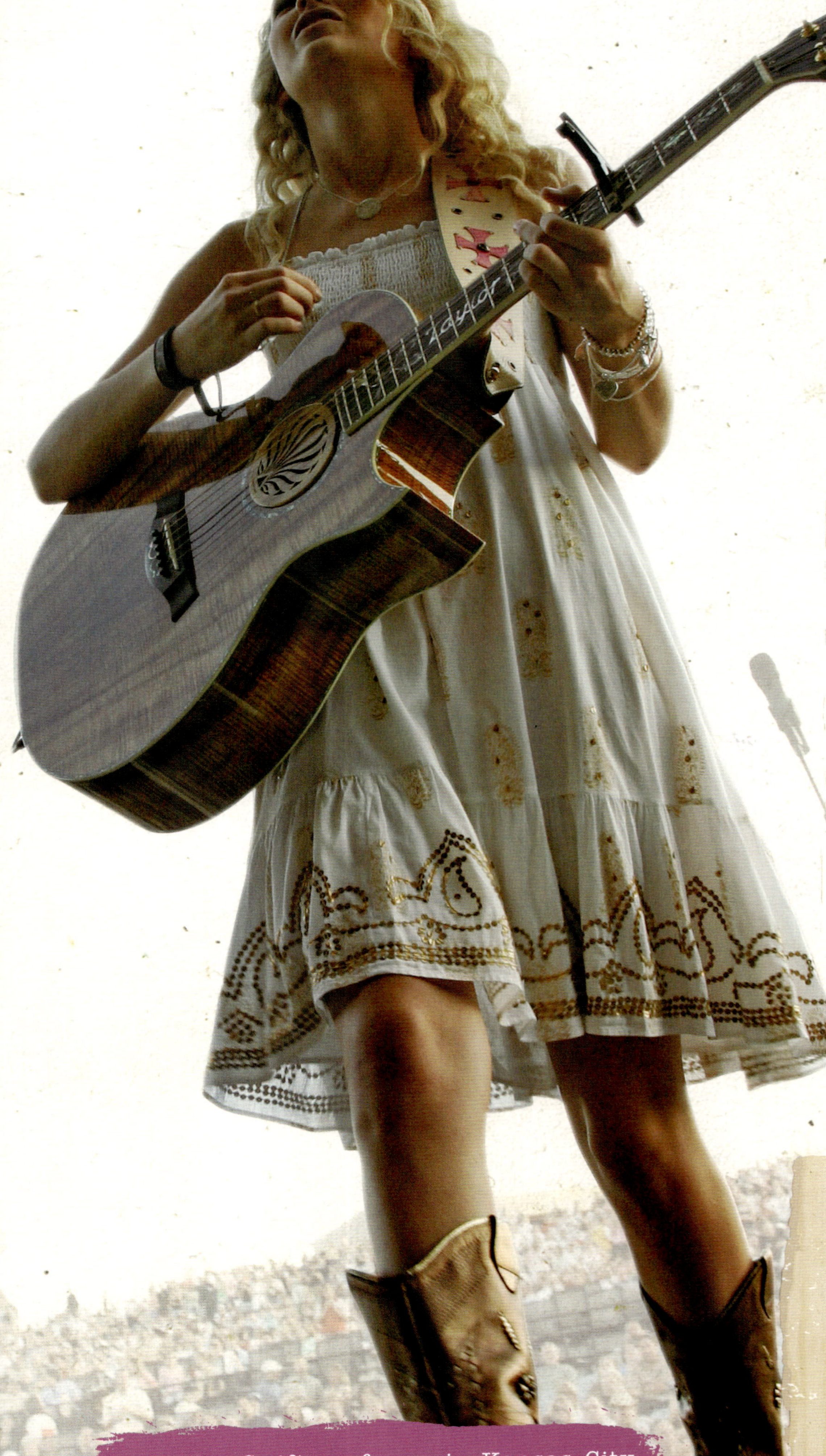

Over the years she came to feel more and more strongly that she wanted to make country music of her own. Taylor took every opportunity to perform at small venues around town, including karaoke clubs, and was always popular. She took extra-curricular lessons in singing, acting, musical theatre and playing guitar. Her parents too began to think this interest might be rather more than a pastime. Taylor soon became convinced that she had to get to Nashville - the world capital of the country music scene, to turn her dreams into reality. Badgering her parents to make the move 700 miles away, Andrea finally compromised by agreeing to take Taylor to Nashville on weekends and holidays. During her frequent trips to Nashville, things were really starting to happen and eventually the buzz around Taylor paid off when she was offered a development deal by RCA which would give her sponsorship and opportunities to record. With something solid to build Taylor and her family took the brave decision to relocate permanently to Nashville. Shortly after, she was offered a record deal with Big Machine Records and in October 2006, when she was just 16, released *Taylor Swift*, the album.

BREAKING RECORDS

Taylor's eponymous debut album introduced her to the world and went on to spend 157 weeks on the Billboard 200 chart, making it the longest-charting album of the first decade of the new millennium. The album also topped the Billboard Top Country Albums chart for 24 weeks and went on to be multi-platinum.

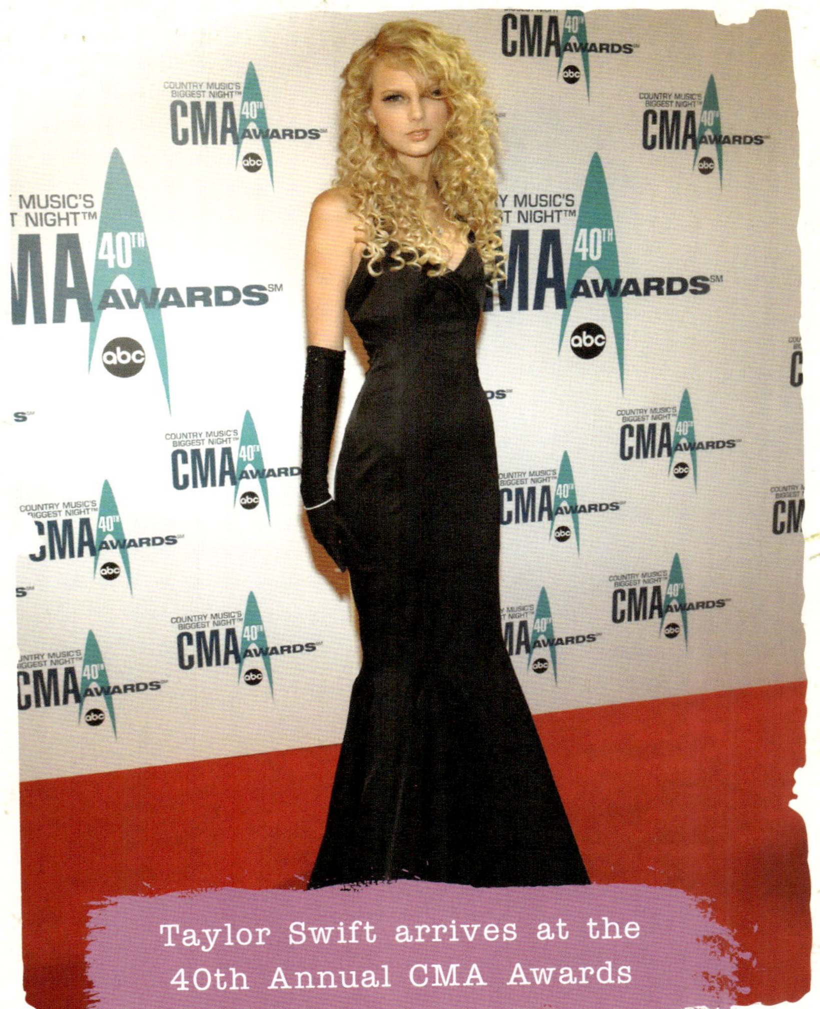

Taylor Swift arrives at the 40th Annual CMA Awards

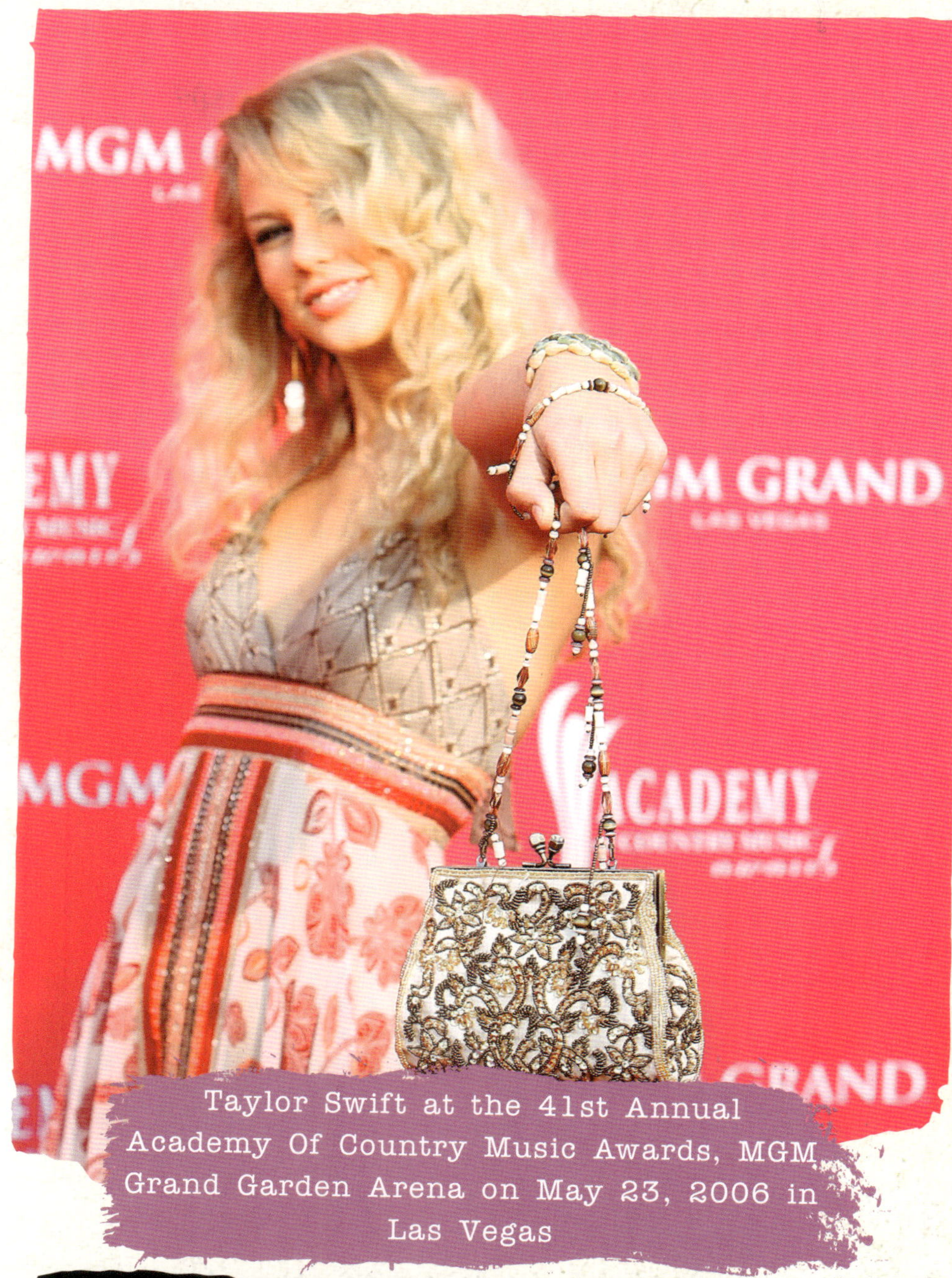

Taylor Swift at the 41st Annual Academy Of Country Music Awards, MGM Grand Garden Arena on May 23, 2006 in Las Vegas

By modernising and rebooting the country music tradition of telling stories about longing and regret, Taylor engaged and energised a new generation of young women who were touched by her often-confessional lyrics and narrative themes. Songs like Teardrops on My Guitar, Tim McGraw and Our Song gave fair warning that she was into 'relationship' themes of all types, whether singing wistfully about doomed love, or bitterly about betrayal, Taylor has gone on to nail the 'heartbreak anthem' genre.

To go along with her youthful and innocent lyrics, Taylor's debut era was characterised by her tight blonde curls, classic smoky eyes, cowboy boots and floaty summer dresses. She was rarely seen performing without her beloved guitar.

By the end of 2008, the *Taylor Swift* album had sold more than three million copies and proved that Taylor had cross-over appeal –the then 19-year-old even scored a Grammy nomination in 2008 for 'Best New Artist' — although she lost out to Amy Winehouse on the night.

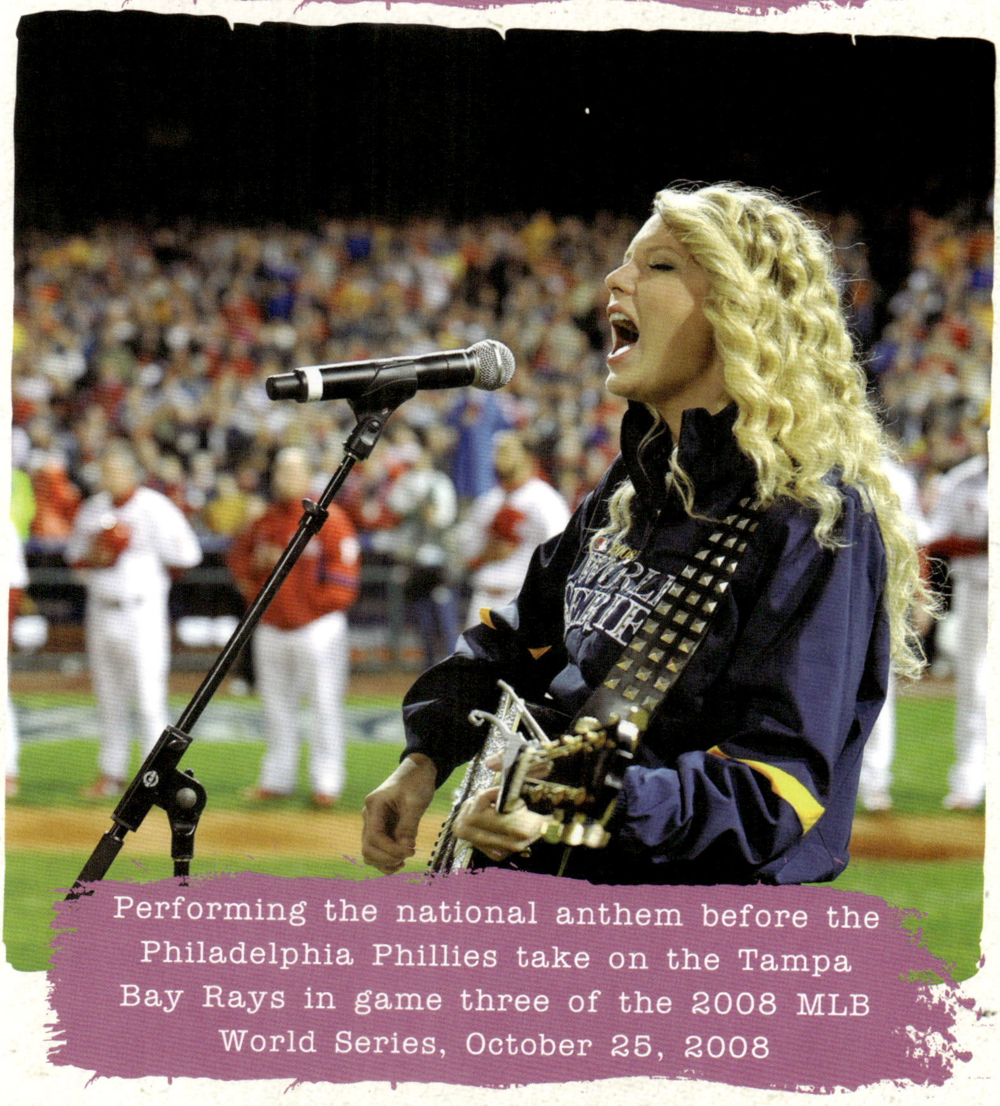

Performing the national anthem before the Philadelphia Phillies take on the Tampa Bay Rays in game three of the 2008 MLB World Series, October 25, 2008

THE FEARLESS ERA 2008

Wildest dreams...

Despite not winning the Grammy for Best New Artist, her presence on the list was enough to catapult her into public consciousness. Now eighteen, Taylor moved into a penthouse apartment of her own in Nashville and was enjoying life, but most importantly she was hard at work writing her highly anticipated follow up album entitled Fearless. During this time, the media became interested in everything about her, particularly her love life.

The young country star thought long and hard about a title which would encapsulate her new collection of songs. 'I thought about my personal definition of 'fearless' and, to me, it doesn't mean that you don't have any fears, it means that you have a lot of fears, but you jump anyway.'

The album debuted at #1 on the Billboard 200 chart and topped the charts for 11 non-consecutive weeks which was longer than any other album that decade. Its two most successful tracks — Love Story and You Belong With Me — gained huge traction in the digital market, bringing Taylor to a wider mainstream audience and helping her break out from the country music scene.

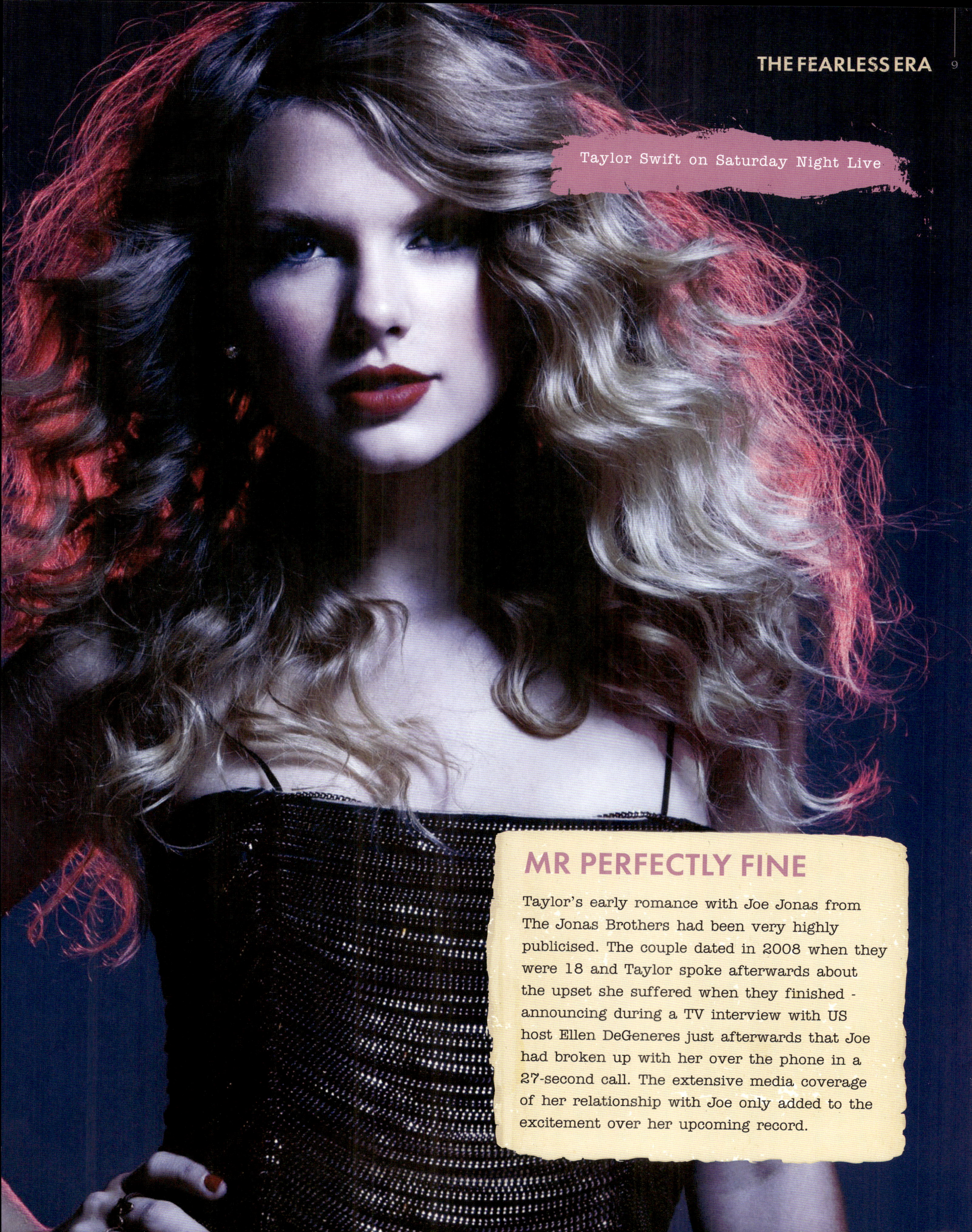

MR PERFECTLY FINE

Taylor's early romance with Joe Jonas from The Jonas Brothers had been very highly publicised. The couple dated in 2008 when they were 18 and Taylor spoke afterwards about the upset she suffered when they finished - announcing during a TV interview with US host Ellen DeGeneres just afterwards that Joe had broken up with her over the phone in a 27-second call. The extensive media coverage of her relationship with Joe only added to the excitement over her upcoming record.

Taylor received huge praise for the honesty and vulnerability she displayed in her 'mature' lyrics, which chronicled the highs and lows of teenage emotions and relationships. This was all hugely satisfying for Taylor, who had written seven of the tracks herself and co-written the others. Fearless helped Taylor to graduate from 'singer-songwriter prodigy to singer songwriter superstar' according to respected rock critic Pierre Perone.

Taylor also went through a physical transformation to match her more refined and mature writing style. She swapped out her trusty cowboy boots for gold, sparkly fringe dresses and big Romeo and Juliet style ballgowns. She also started painting her lucky number 13 on the back of her hand. Taylor still wore her signature curly hair, but introduced a red lip, a style that would become a go-to for the singer. She also established herself as a respected performer with her shows becoming more theatrical and intricate.

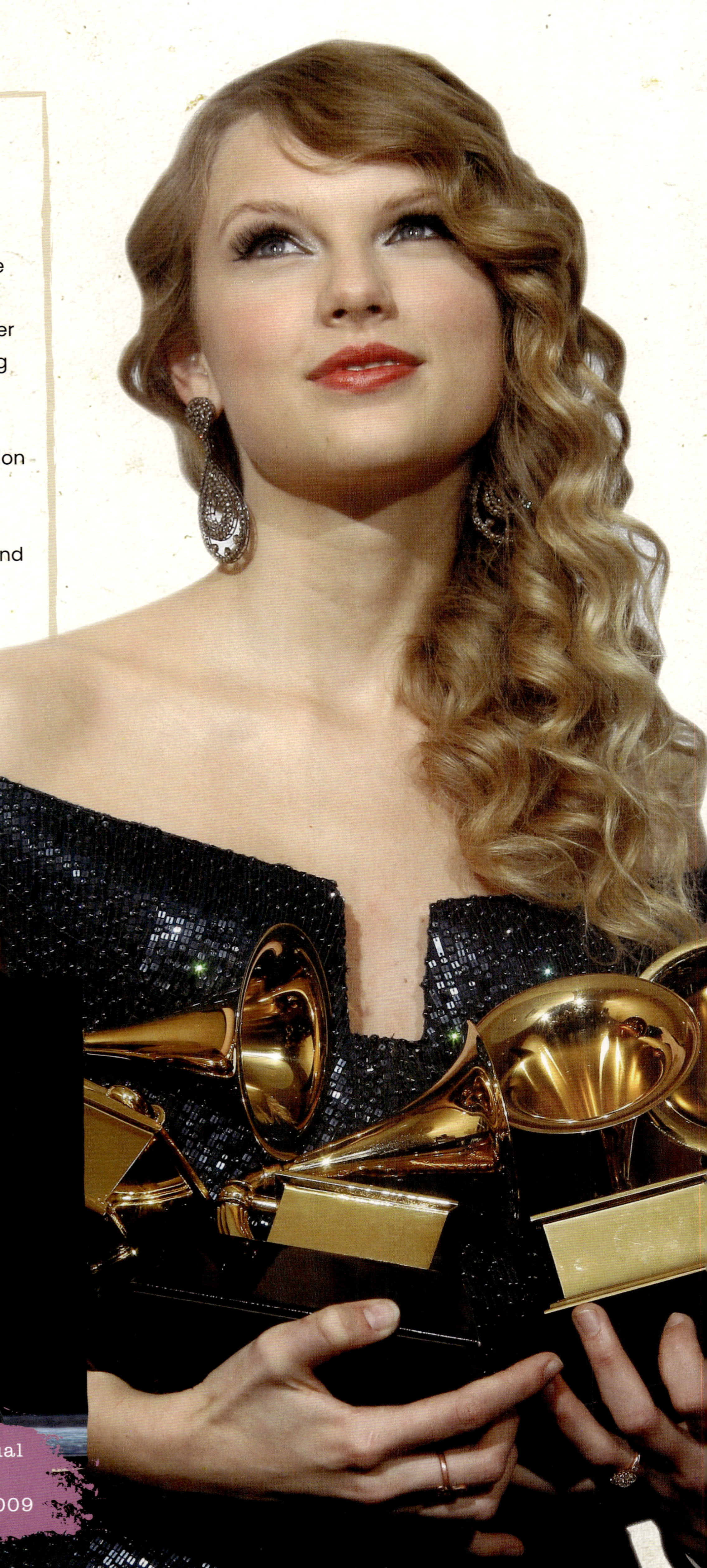

Taylor Swift performs at the 43rd Annual Country Music Association Awards in Nashville, Tennessee on November 11, 2009

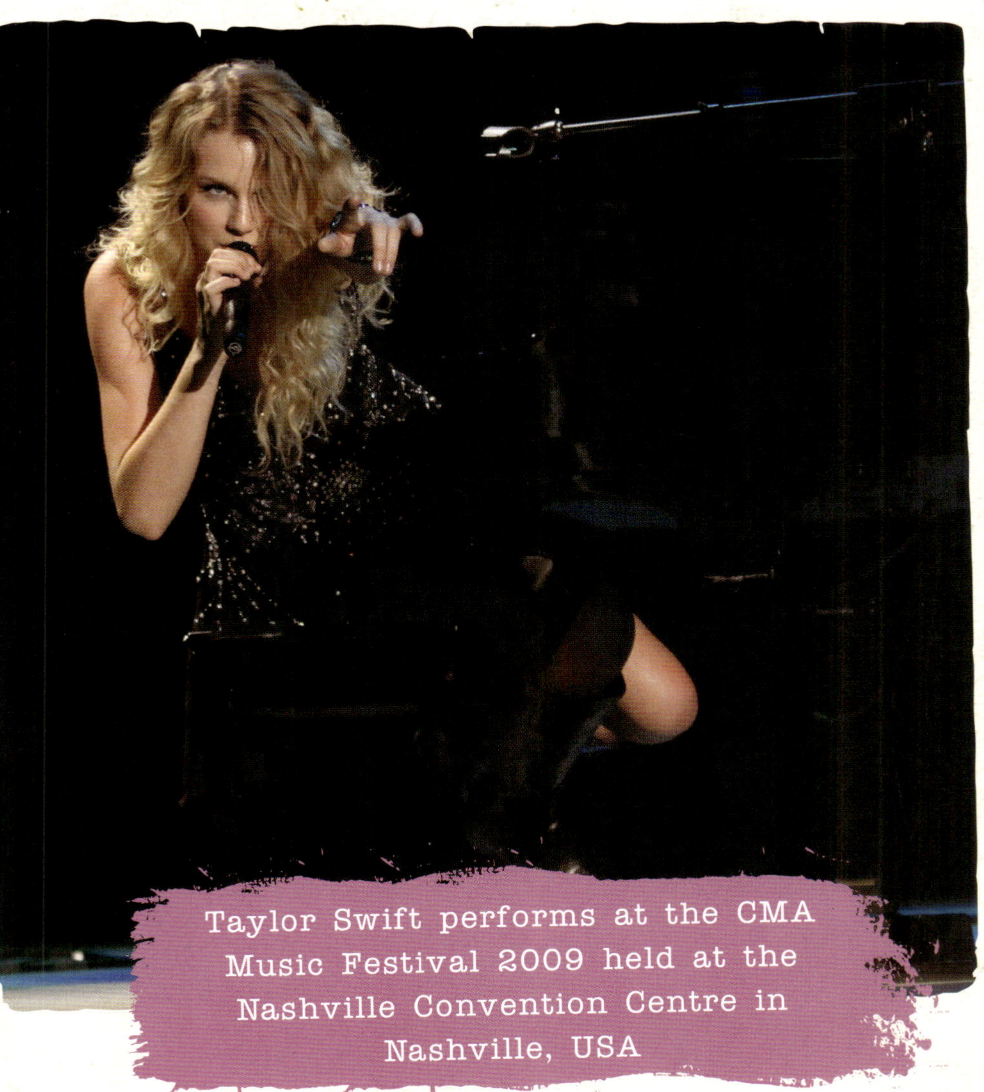

Taylor Swift performs at the CMA Music Festival 2009 held at the Nashville Convention Centre in Nashville, USA

But amid her success, Taylor became embroiled in one of the biggest award show controversies in music history. It was of course the incident with rapper and record producer Kanye West at the 2009 MTV Video Music Awards.

BAD BLOOD

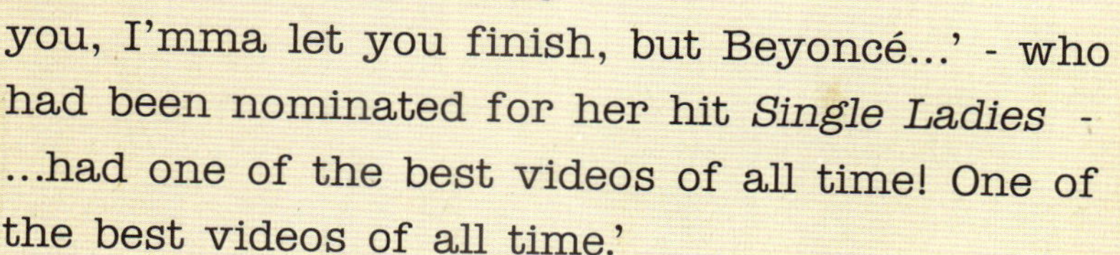

Taylor just had won Best Female Video for her song *You Belong With Me* and was on stage making her acceptance speech when she was suddenly interrupted by Kanye. The rapper wrestled the microphone away from her, saying 'Yo, Taylor, I'm really happy for you, I'mma let you finish, but Beyoncé…' - who had been nominated for her hit *Single Ladies* - …had one of the best videos of all time! One of the best videos of all time.'

The incident completely ruined Taylor's moment of celebration for one of her first big mainstream awards. Kanye gave her back the microphone and walked offstage leaving Taylor mouth open in shock, clearly at a loss for what to do. Later in the evening, Taylor performed an epic rendition of *You Belong With Me* and was invited on stage by Beyoncé to finish her speech. The US President Barack Obama even got involved, calling Kanye a 'jackass' when he was asked for his opinion on the situation.

13 is Taylor's lucky number. She paints it on her hand before a show and so do her fans.

Speaking to MTV in 2009, she explained: 'I was born on the 13th. I turned 13 on Friday the 13th. My first album went gold in 13 weeks. My first number one song had a 13-second intro. Every time I've won an award I've been seated in either the 13th seat, the 13th row, the 13th section or row M, which is the 13th letter. Basically whenever a 13 comes up in my life, it's a good thing.'

Taylor wasn't going to be brought down by these events and just a few months later at the 2010 Grammy awards, *Fearless* won four of the prizes, including the hotly contested Album of the Year – one of the most prestigious awards in the music industry. Taylor had just turned twenty and was the youngest person ever to have won the award.

THE SPEAK NOW ERA 2010

Better than Revenge

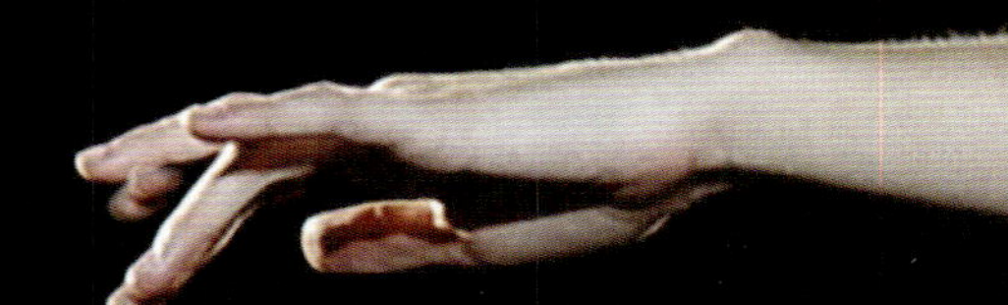

Never one to sit back on her laurels, Taylor had also begun working on her third album *Speak Now* almost as soon as *Fearless* had been released.

Speak Now marked an important point in Taylor's career by documenting her transition from adolescent to adult star, now ready to speak her truth.

Taylor Swift playing a sold-out crowd of over 51,000 fans on her 'Speak Now' World Tour, Lincoln Financial Field in her home state of Pennsylvania

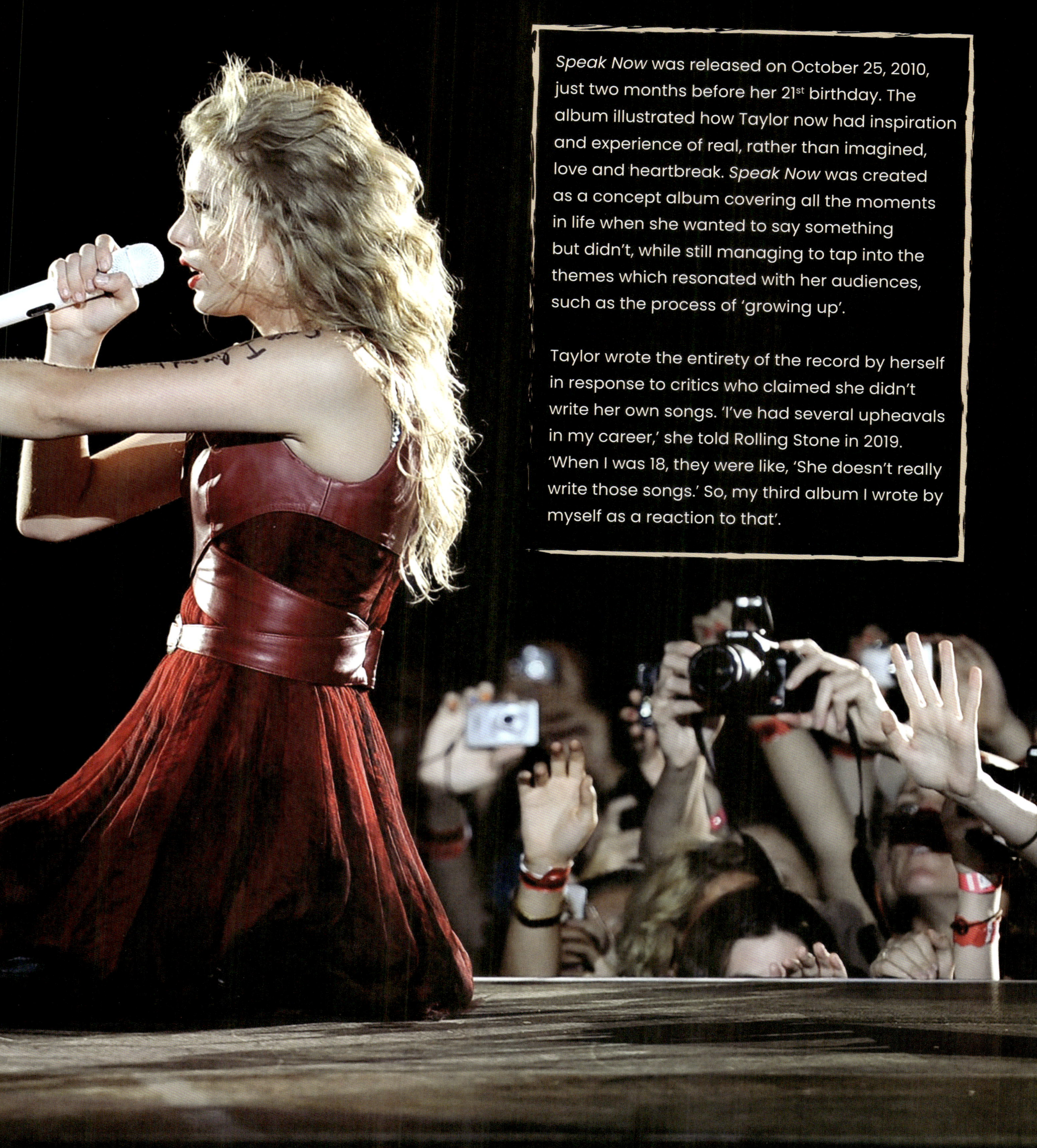

Speak Now was released on October 25, 2010, just two months before her 21st birthday. The album illustrated how Taylor now had inspiration and experience of real, rather than imagined, love and heartbreak. *Speak Now* was created as a concept album covering all the moments in life when she wanted to say something but didn't, while still managing to tap into the themes which resonated with her audiences, such as the process of 'growing up'.

Taylor wrote the entirety of the record by herself in response to critics who claimed she didn't write her own songs. 'I've had several upheavals in my career,' she told Rolling Stone in 2019. 'When I was 18, they were like, 'She doesn't really write those songs.' So, my third album I wrote by myself as a reaction to that'.

Speak Now was a truly personal and confessional album that focused on that transitional period between 'adolescence and adulthood, innocence and understanding, country and pop'. The album also marked a definite departure from Taylor's roots and was decidedly more 'pop' and less 'country' than her previous work.

Throughout her career Taylor has always written about what she knows – never trying to sound or write as older than she is. In that way, and despite her growing fame, she has always shared many of the emotions that other women of her age have experienced.

Speak Now was also the first album to cover numerous celebrity boyfriends. Taylor notably dated John Mayer and Taylor Lautner during this era, and remnants from her heartbreak with Joe Jonas also appear in the record.

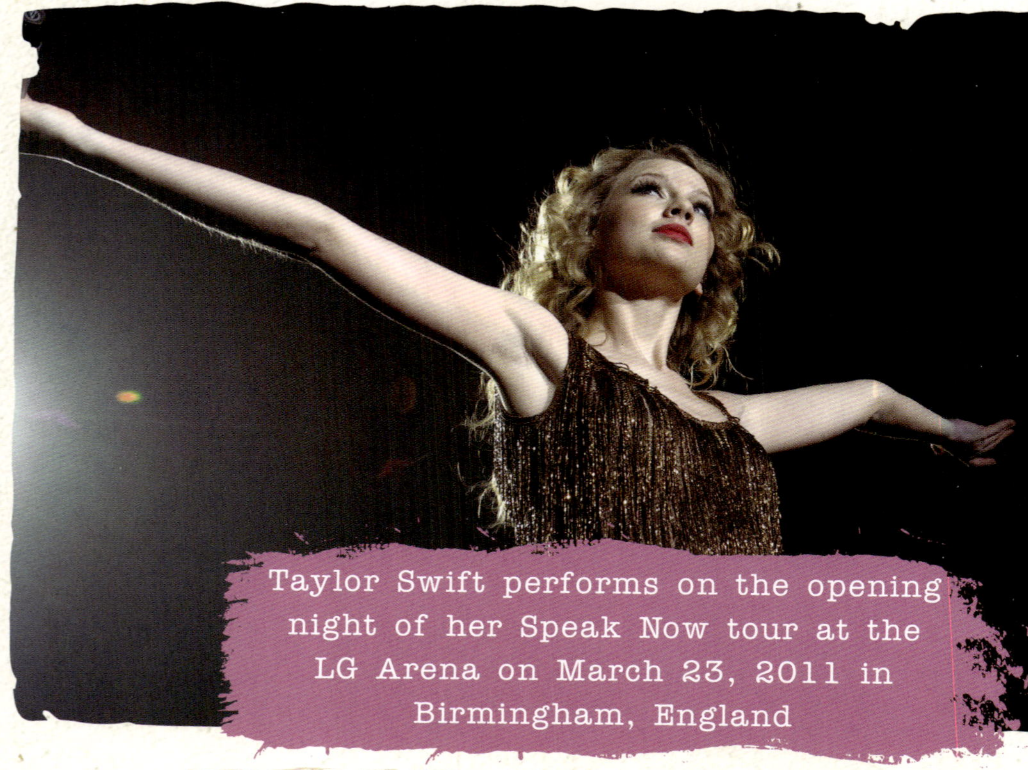

Taylor Swift performs on the opening night of her Speak Now tour at the LG Arena on March 23, 2011 in Birmingham, England

Not surprisingly, Speak Now was a massive success. In its first week, the album sold more than a million copies and went on to become triple platinum, making #1 in the US, Canada, Australia, and New Zealand. Six singles were released to support the album, with *Mine* and *Back to December* making the top 10 of the Billboard Hot 100.

After the album's release, Taylor embarked on her Speak Now World Tour, visiting 17 countries across Asia, Europe, North America, and Australasia between February 2011 and March 2012. Again scenery, costume and production values were high and theatrical, while Taylor also managed to create moments of spontaneity which enchanted audiences.

It was another massively successful tour, with critics praising everything from its sheer visual impact to Taylor's performance and connection with the audience.

It became the highest-grossing female and solo tour of 2011, earning over $120 million.

The "Speak Now" era was undoubtedly defined by its magical and theatrical aspects, Taylor's purple, ethereal, 'fairy tale' inspired dresses, alongside her lucky number 13 on her hand.

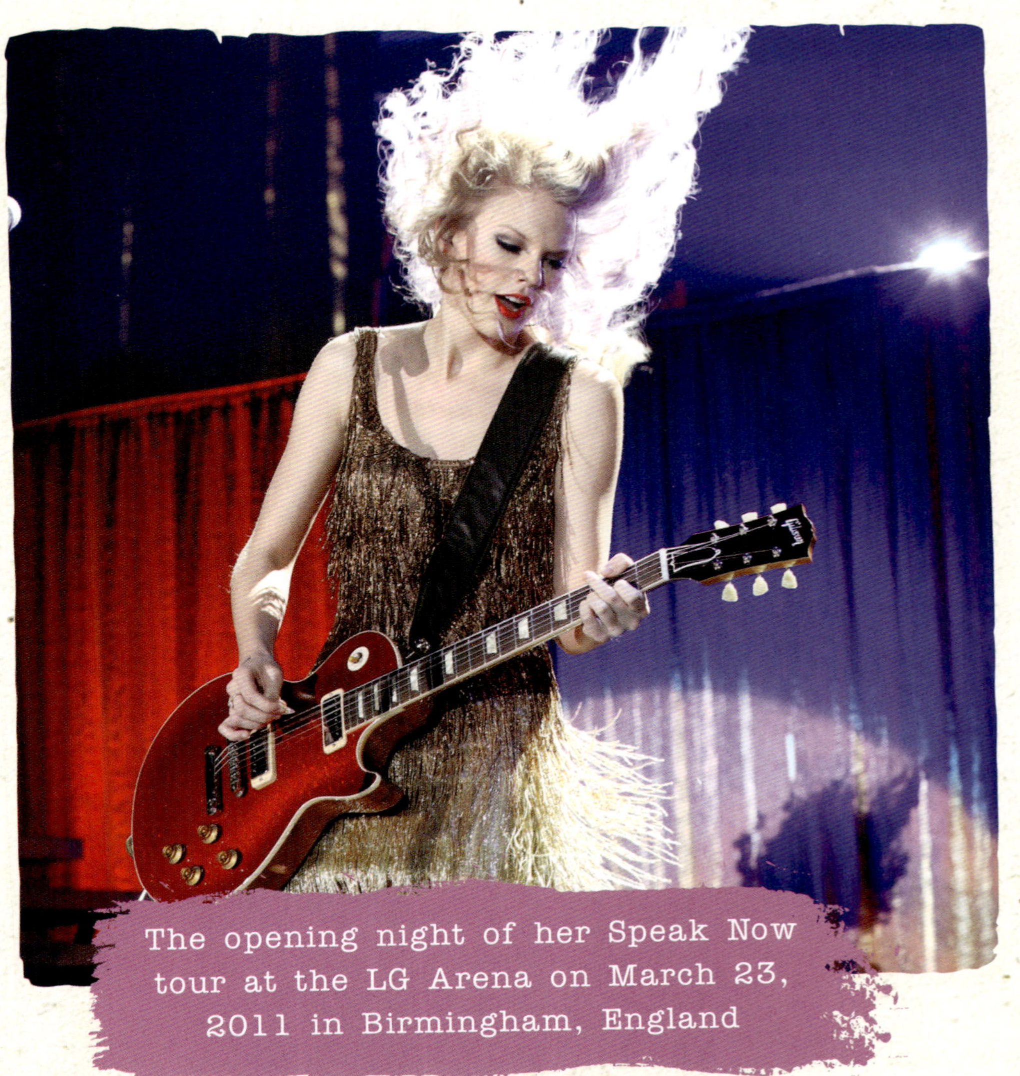

The opening night of her Speak Now tour at the LG Arena on March 23, 2011 in Birmingham, England

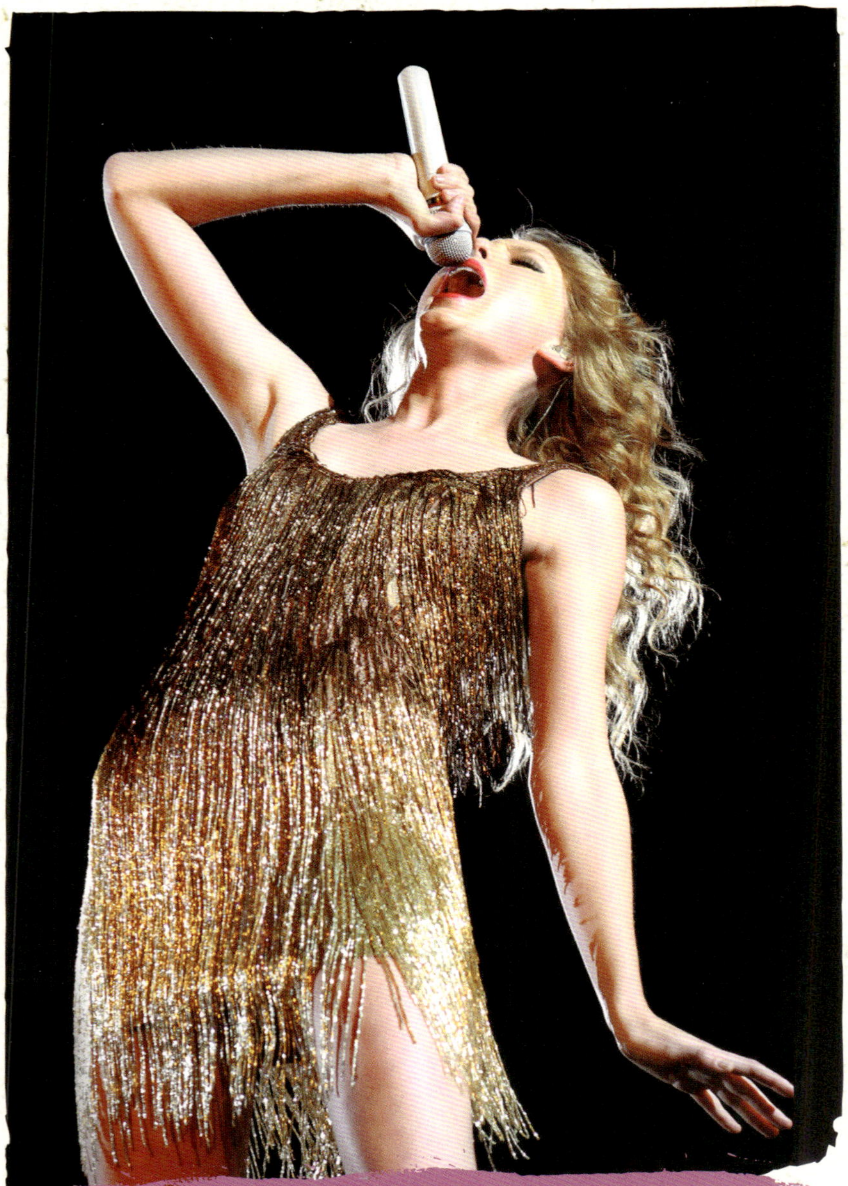

WE ARE NEVER EVER EVER GETTING BACK TOGETHER...

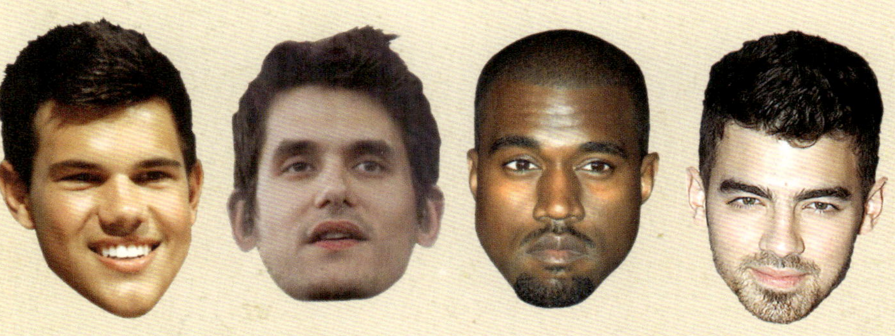

'Back To December', is a ballad about regretting breaking up with Taylor Lautner.

'Dear John', is an open letter asking John Mayer whether he should have messed with her heart so young (he was 32, and she was 19).

'Innocent' covers her reaction to the Kanye's interruption at the VMA's in 2009.

Taylor also wrote a song dedicated to Joe Jonas entitled 'Last Kiss' on her next album which included a 27-second-long introduction, the same length as the phone call where he broke up with her.

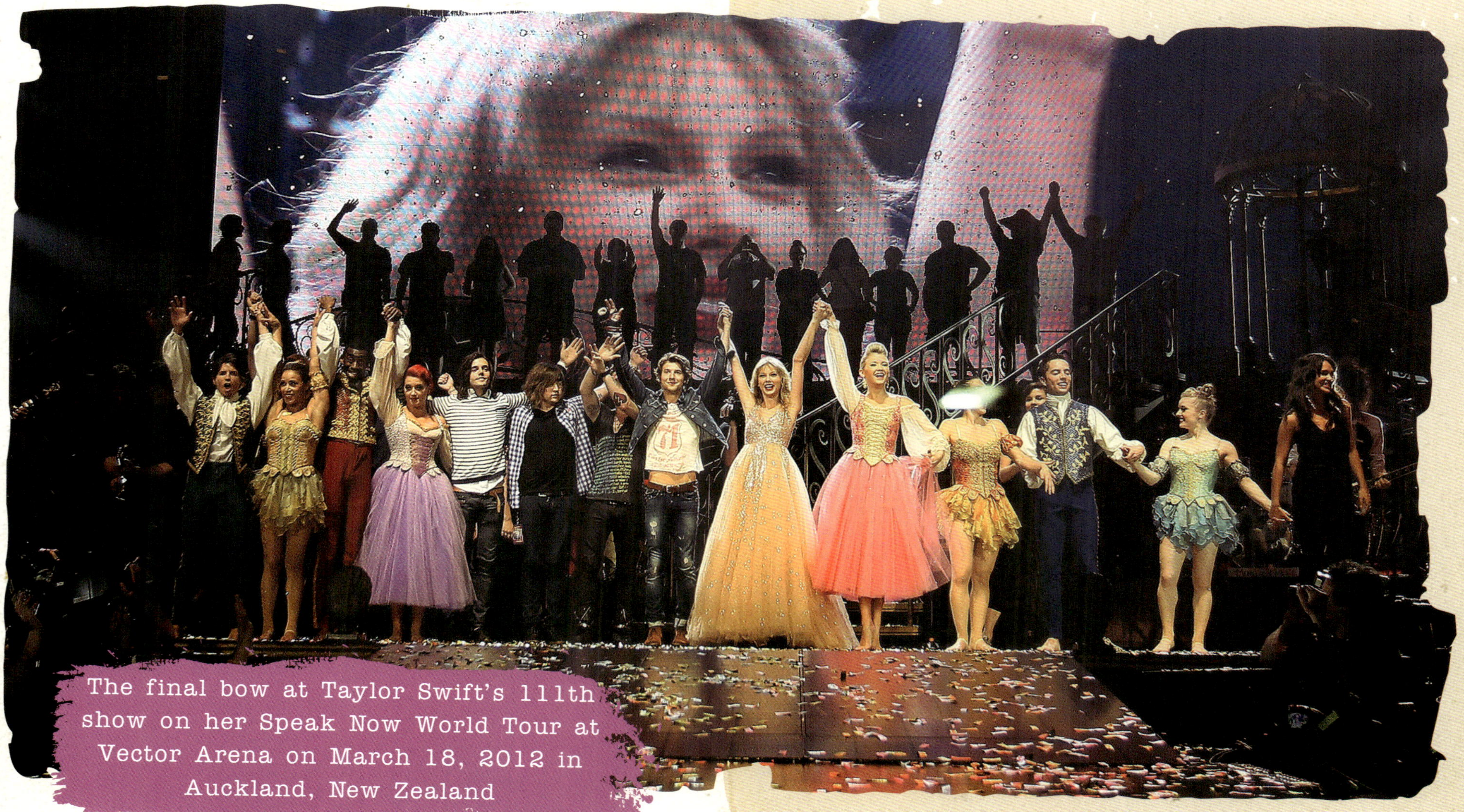

Taylor Swift performs on the opening night of her Speak Now tour

The final bow at Taylor Swift's 111th show on her Speak Now World Tour at Vector Arena on March 18, 2012 in Auckland, New Zealand

THE RED ERA

2012 *Everything has changed...*

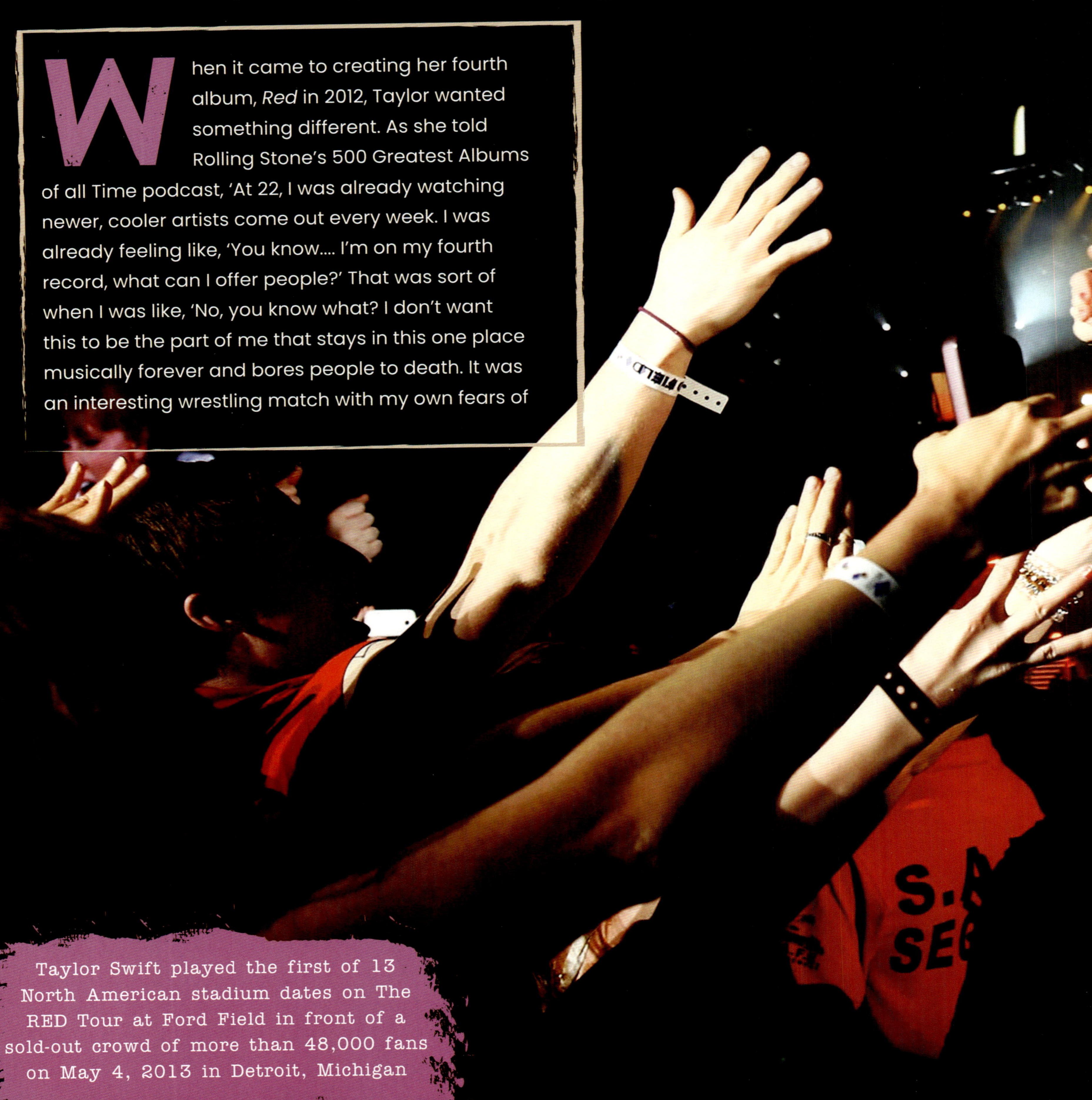

When it came to creating her fourth album, *Red* in 2012, Taylor wanted something different. As she told Rolling Stone's 500 Greatest Albums of all Time podcast, 'At 22, I was already watching newer, cooler artists come out every week. I was already feeling like, 'You know.... I'm on my fourth record, what can I offer people?' That was sort of when I was like, 'No, you know what? I don't want this to be the part of me that stays in this one place musically forever and bores people to death. It was an interesting wrestling match with my own fears of remaining stagnant that made *Red* the kind of joy ride that it ended up being'.

The stage was set for Taylor to begin her transition to the mainstream pop charts. This she did with her fourth album *Red* – the album which boldly fulfilled Taylor's wish to move from country star to major league player and one of the most successful artists in the world.

Style: Begin Again...

The Red era in many ways represented a turning point in Taylor's life and career, as she experimented with new genres such as mainstream pop, rock, and even EDM and dubstep.

Taylor swapped out her usual glittery gowns for high-waisted shorts, striped shirts, and vintage dresses — and famously ditched her signature bouncy curls for sleek, straight locks, to reflect her shift in sound and themes in her new album. She also traded her lucky number 13 for her signature red lip in honour of her record. Taylor was signalling to everyone that she has grown up and was ready to be the biggest superstar in the world.

The album's title 'Red' is a reference to the extreme, 'red', emotions that Taylor experienced during the album's conception phase, when she described feeling 'intense love, intense frustration, jealousy, confusion …[where] there's nothing in between'.

The pop hooks in tracks such as *I Knew You Were Trouble* and *We Are Never Ever Getting Back Together* were phenomenal, while the lyrics were generally among the most insightful, she had ever produced.

I knew you were trouble…

Taylor's love life continued to fascinate the media and alike, including her well-publicised romance with actor Jake Gyllenhaal. Taylor dated Jake, 10 years her senior, for a couple of months at the end of 2010 before calling it a day in January 2011. Many of the songs on Red were thought to be based on him, including *The Moment I Knew*, rumoured to be about the time he didn't show up at her 21st birthday party, *We Are Never Ever Getting Back Together*, and *All Too Well*.

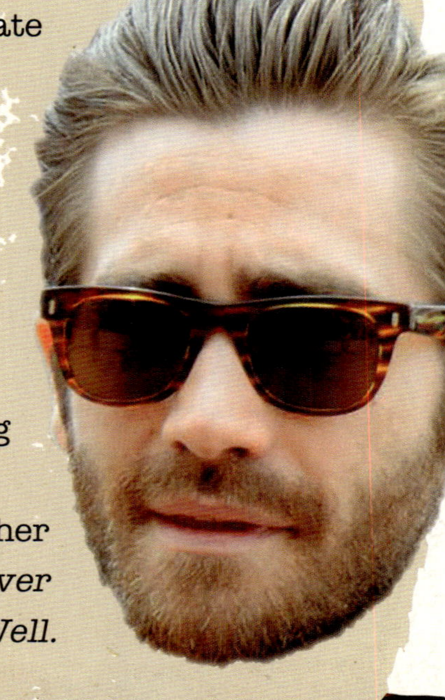

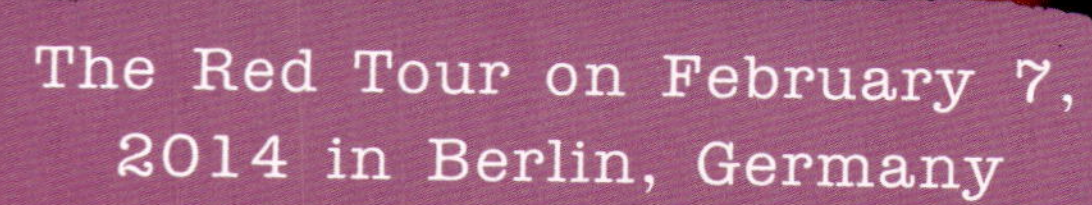

The Red Tour on February 7, 2014 in Berlin, Germany

Taylor Swift accepts the award for Entertainer of the Year at the 47th Annual Academy Of Country Music Awards held at the MGM Grand Garden Arena on April 1, 2012 in Las Vegas

Red sold 1.2 million copies during its first week on sale in the US – more than any album in a single week since 2002. By the following year it had achieved worldwide sales of six million. The album spent seven weeks at the top of the US Billboard 200 album chart, giving Taylor the accolade of being the first female artist and only the second act since The Beatles to have three consecutive albums at number one for at least six weeks.

It gave Taylor her first #1 album in the UK, while also topping the charts in Australia, Canada, and New Zealand.

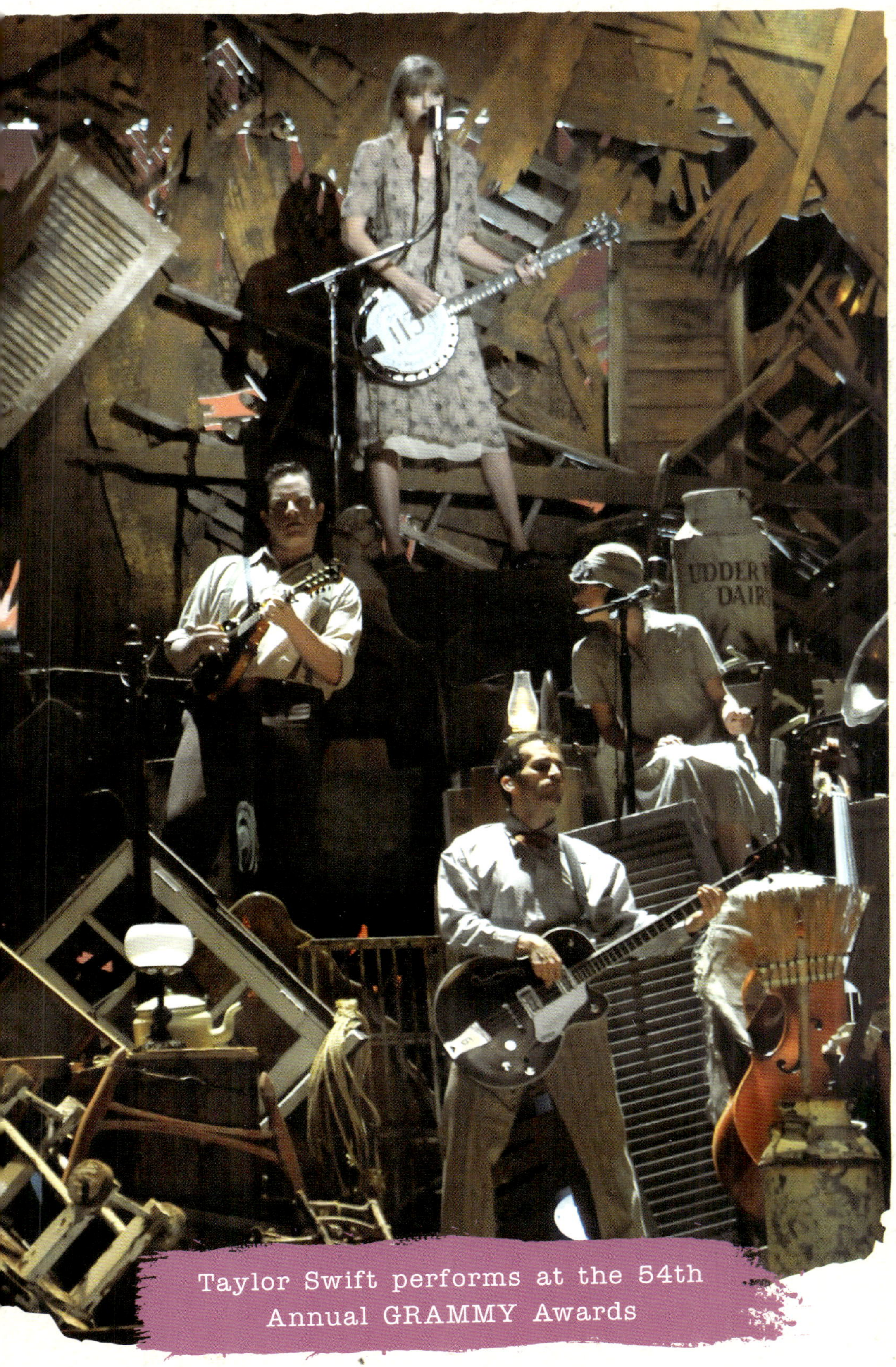

Taylor Swift performs at the 54th Annual GRAMMY Awards

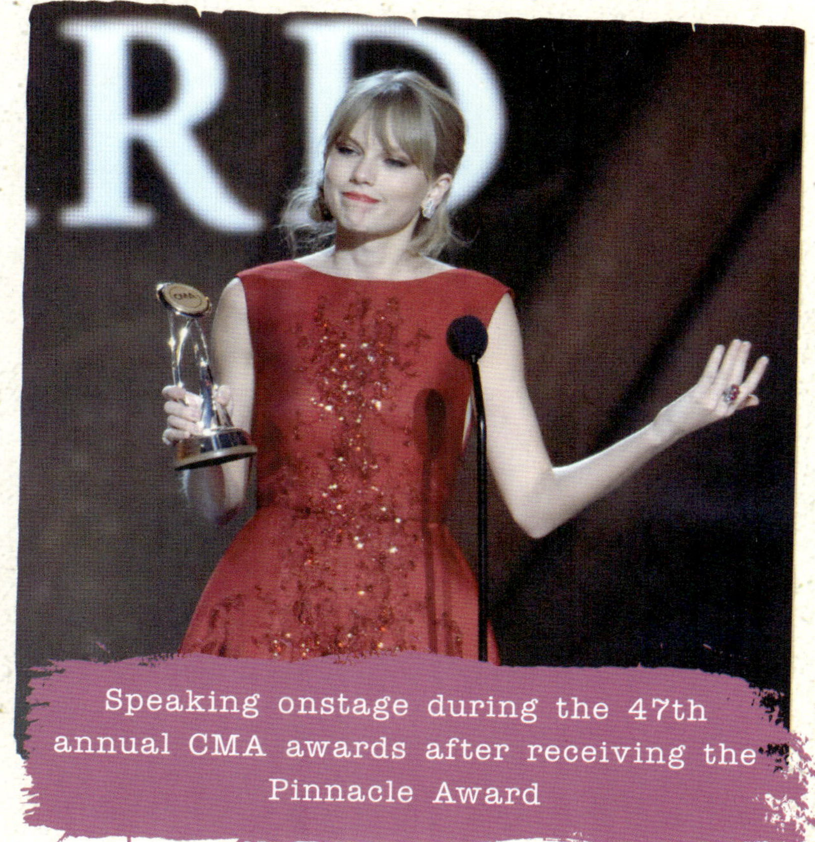

Speaking onstage during the 47th annual CMA awards after receiving the Pinnacle Award

Taylor promoted the album with the colossal Red Tour which ran from March 2013 to June 2014, becoming the most successful tour by a country artist of all time, grossing $150 million. It was a massive production featuring 15 dancers, four backing singers, a seven-piece band, multi-level stages, hydraulics, confetti showers and costume changes galore.

In all, *Red* earned over 50 accolades, including four nominations at the 56th Annual *Grammy Awards*. Also in 2013, aged just 23, Taylor was presented with the highest award in country music, the CMA 'Pinnacle Award'.

Now recognised and respected as a musician, Taylor was named Woman of the Year by Billboard in 2012 – making her the youngest artist to receive that honour – listed by Forbes as the highest earning star aged under 30.

She had reached the top of the mountain as far as country music goes.

What next?

STELLAR SINGLE
Never Ever Getting Back Together

This upbeat pop rock tune about not getting back together with an ex quickly gained popularity and rose to number one by making one of the biggest leaps up the charts in history, moving up 72 spots in a single week to give Taylor her first number one on the Billboard Hot 100 chart.

THE 1989 ERA

2014 *Just Shake It Off!*

Having reportedly been 'devastated' when Red didn't pick up the Grammy for Best Album, and in typical Taylor fashion, she simply decided she needed to work a little bit harder. The result was her fifth album, the blockbusting *1989*, titled after the year of her birth. The *1989* record was quite simply a euphoric pop masterpiece.

Its synth-pop tracks – including chart-topping singles *Blank Space and Shake it Off* - ensured Taylor shed her country roots completely and transitioned to a pure pop sound. She worked with co-writers and producers on this album, including Jack Antonoff for the first time.

Breaking records

Topping the Billboard 200 chart for 11 weeks, *1989* became her fourth American #1 album and her third consecutive album to sell above one million copies in its first week - a new record for any artist. With sales of 1.29 million in its first week, *1989* had the biggest seven-day sales of any release since 2002, according to Nielsen SoundScan. *1989* went on to win album of the year at the 2016 Grammy's, making Taylor the first female artist ever to win the prize twice. The album also picked up the Grammy for Best Pop Vocal Album and appeared on several 2010s best albums lists. *Rolling Stone* went on to feature it in their 2020 revised list of the 500 Greatest Albums of All Time.

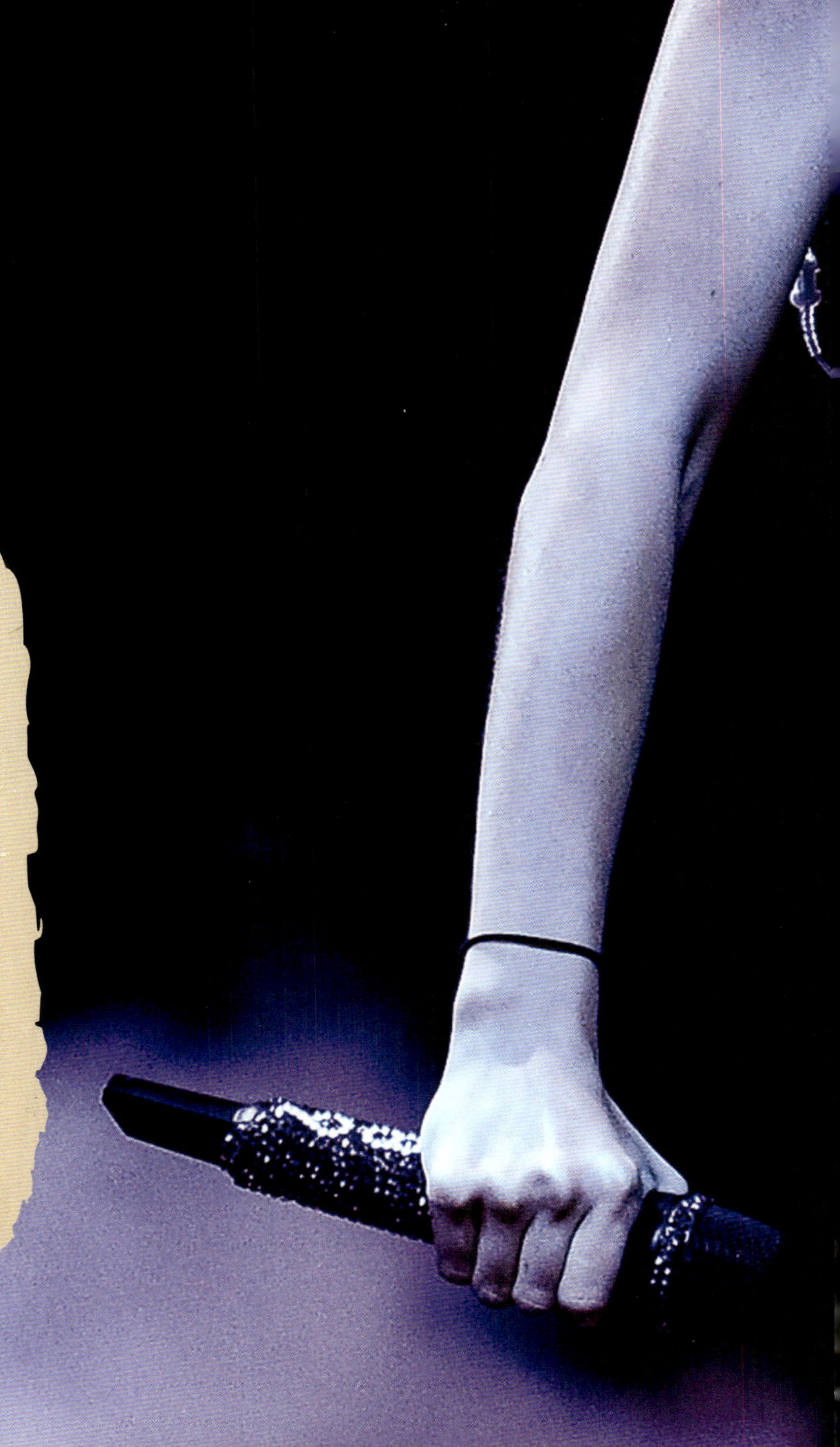

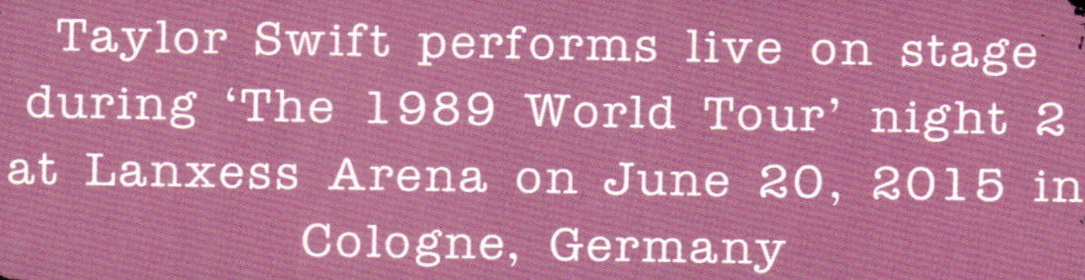

Taylor Swift performs live on stage during 'The 1989 World Tour' night 2 at Lanxess Arena on June 20, 2015 in Cologne, Germany

In several interviews to promote the album Taylor mentioned the idea of a 'rebirth'. Mirroring her transition from country to pop, the "1989" era was also defined by other major changes for the star: she relocated to New York City, cut her hair into a short bob, and, of course, changed up her aesthetic, opting for crop tops, short skirts, and more form-fitting clothes that completed her transformation into a full-blown mega-pop star.

The album's content was a very positive clap back to the criticisms she had begun receiving about her personal life and relationship issues. With her career at an all-time high, Taylor had become an important cultural figure, with people becoming fascinated by her every word, move, and romance.

Things started harmlessly enough with some jokes about Taylor's love life, but quickly morphed into less good-natured comments, depicting Taylor as a mad girlfriend, obsessed with her exes. Taylor who had always been fuelled by a need 'to be thought of as "good"', took the media scrutiny hard. But as usual she used her experience as inspiration for her music.

STELLAR SINGLE
Shake It Off

Calling out all her haters – this was Taylor's catchy retort that she would continue her success without caring what her detractors thought

This single was a #1 in the US and #2 in the UK where it remains her best-selling ever. It stayed at number one on the American charts for four weeks and then remained on the chart in various positions for 50 weeks in total. It went on to receive diamond certification, three Grammy nominations and won a People's Choice Award.

STELLAR SINGLE
Blank Space

This single cemented Taylor's shift to the mainstream and acknowledged her new image that was surfacing because she was becoming known for writing about her exes. Taylor told *Rolling Stone* that *Blank Space* was written as a satire on her perceived image saying she thought, 'OK, this is what you're all saying about me. Let me just write from this character for a second'.

The single picked up three Grammy nominations, The song not only reached number one on Billboard Hot 100 but stayed there for seven weeks.

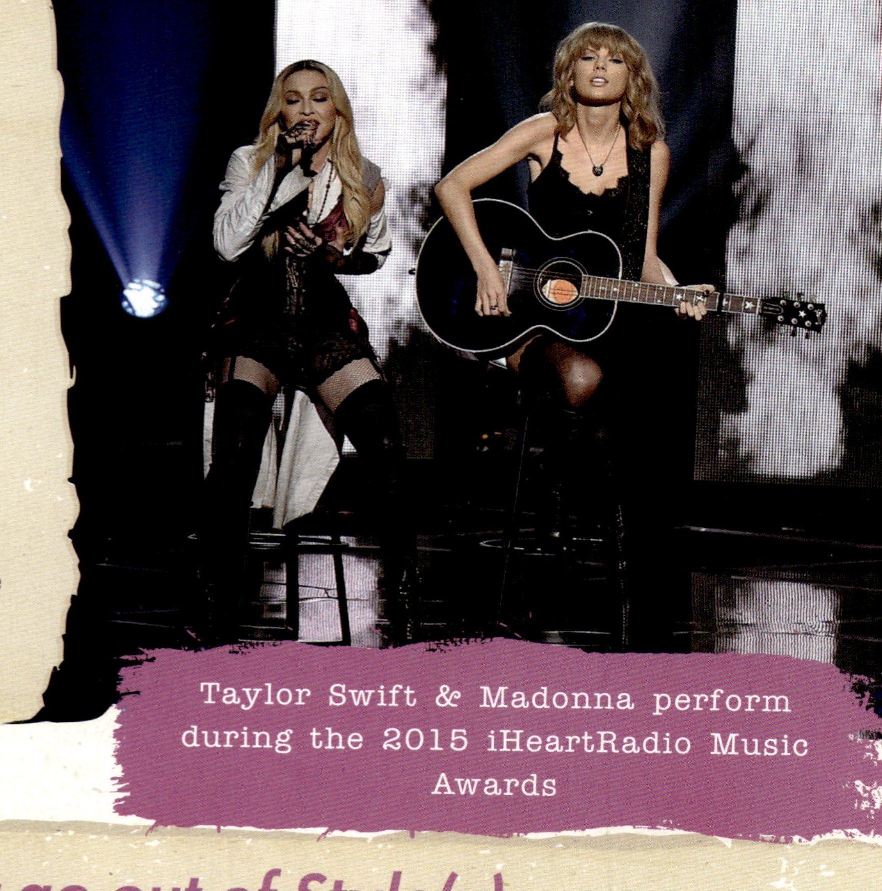

Taylor Swift & Madonna perform during the 2015 iHeartRadio Music Awards

We'll never go out of Style(s)...

When fans got wind of a relationship between Taylor and boyband megastar Harry Styles from One Direction in 2012, they internet went crazy and the hashtag '#Haylor' was trending everywhere. Their time together was short - and is rumoured to have ended with a big row during a New Year's holiday on the British Virgin Islands - but fans got a lot out of it. Both Taylor and Harry subsequently released music believed to be about their time together.

Several of Taylor's tracks have been mentioned as possible Harry-related songs, including *I Wish You Would*, *Style* and *Out of the Woods*.

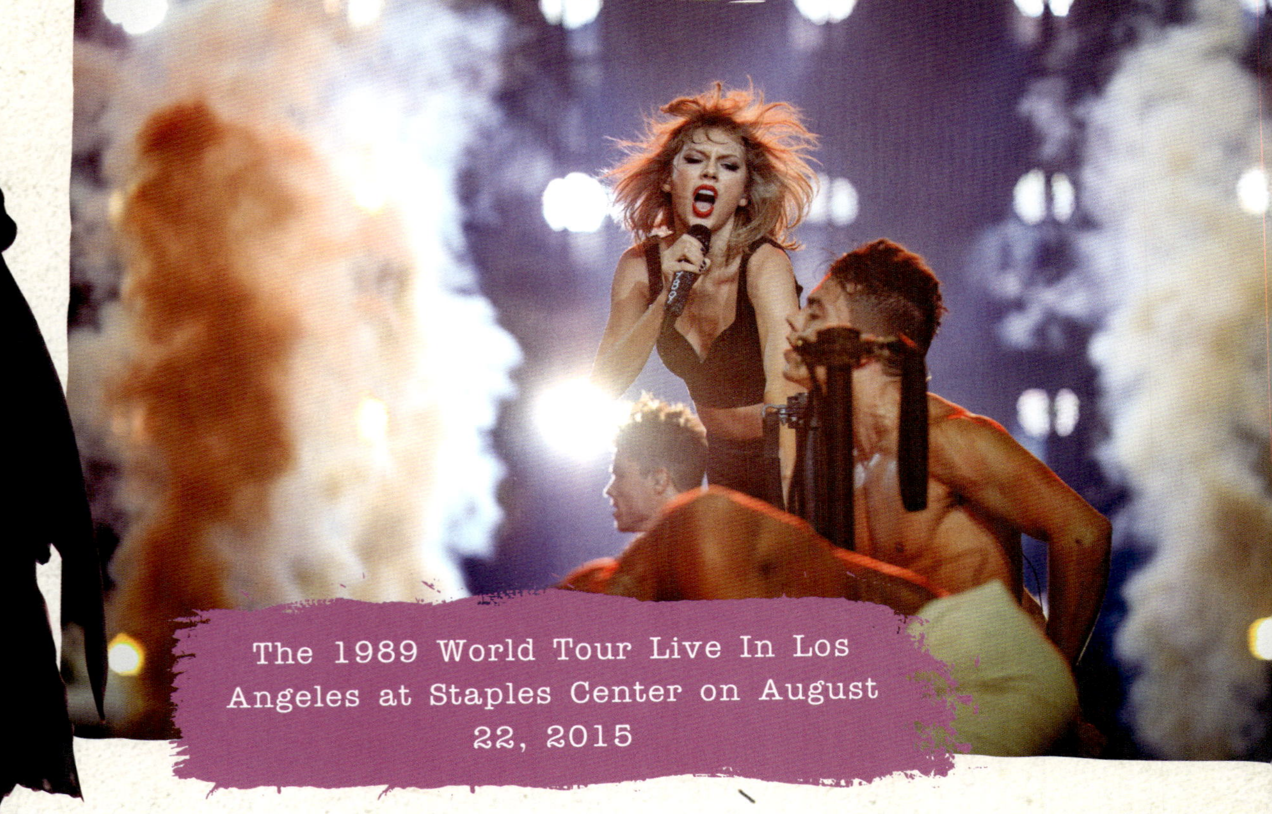

The 1989 World Tour Live In Los Angeles at Staples Center on August 22, 2015

SQUAD GIRLS

Taylor has lots of famous girlfriends who are known in the press as members of her 'squad'. Some of these women featured in Taylor's iconic video for Bad Blood.

Squad members old and new, many of them actresses and models include:

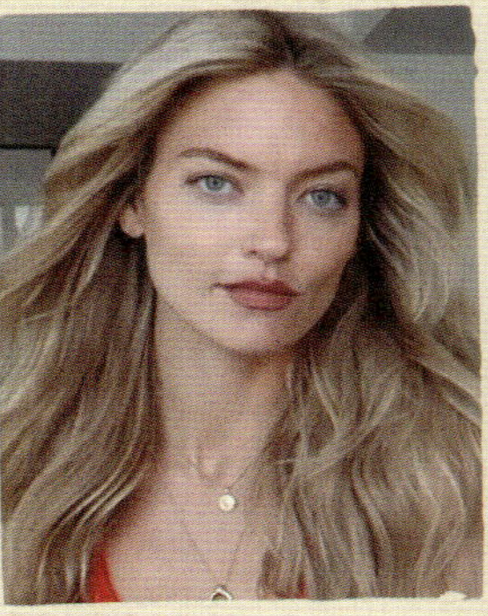

Martha Hunt

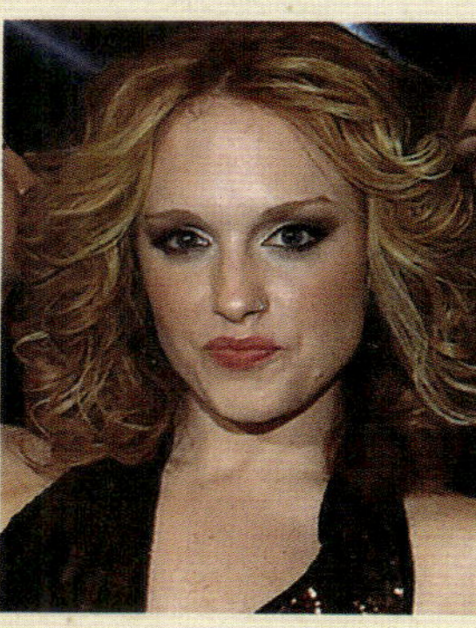

Abigail Anderson

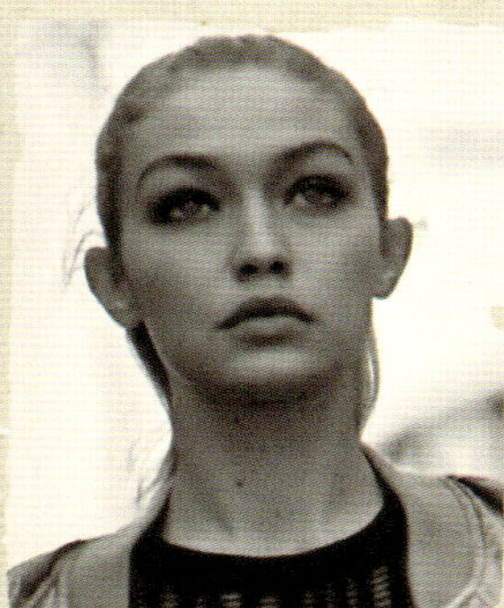

Gigi Hadid

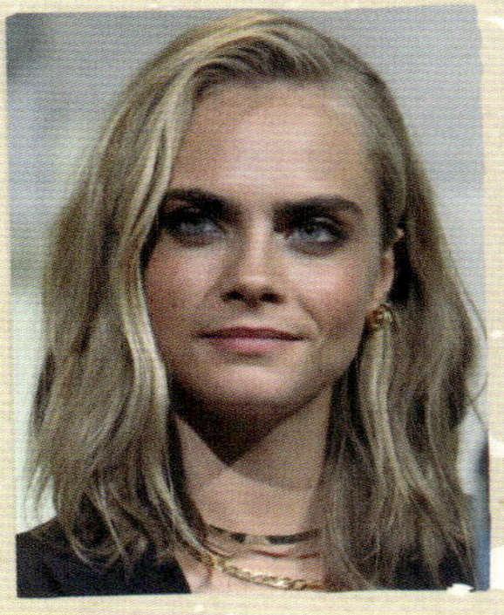

Carla Delevingne

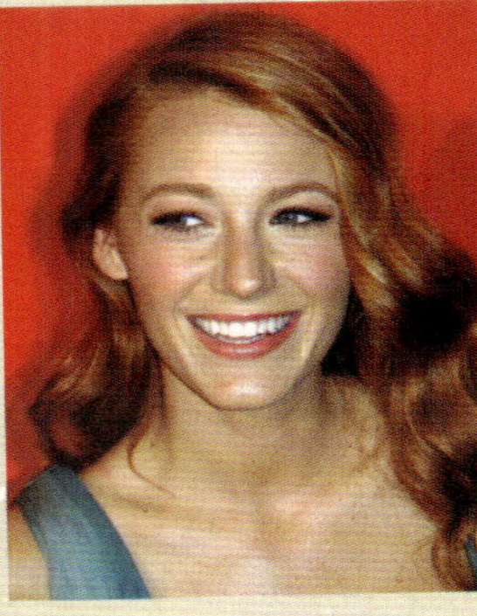

Blake Lively

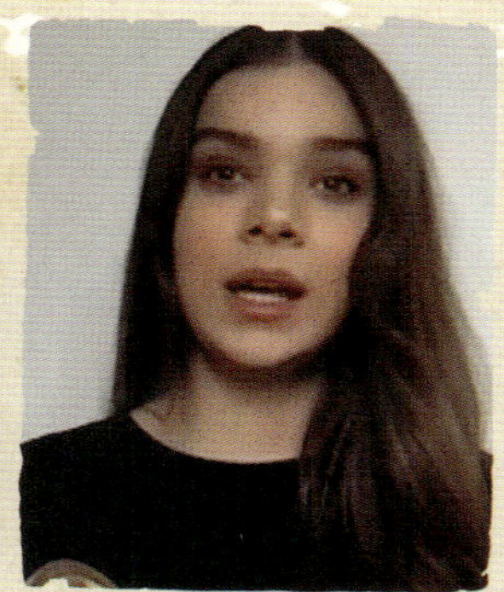

Hailee Steinfeld

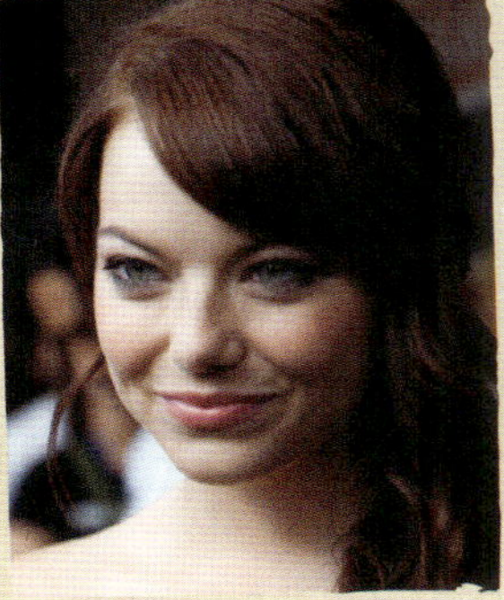

Emma Stone

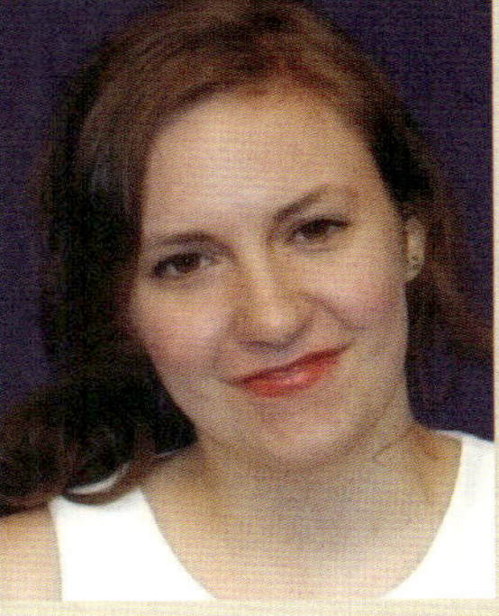

Lena Dunham

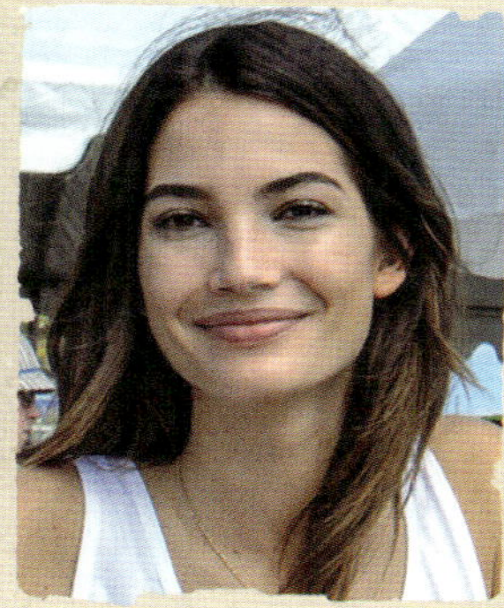

Lily Aldridge

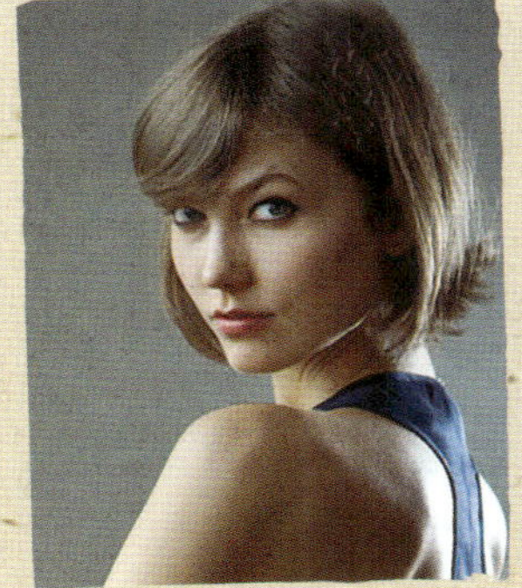

Karlie Kloss

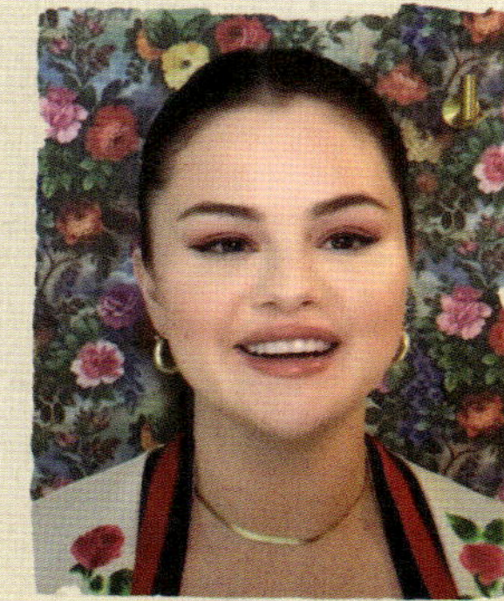

Selena Gomez

Taylor Swift during "The 1989 World Tour" at Levi's Stadium on August 15, 2015 in Santa Clara, California

In addition to her album 1989 becoming one of the most famous pop albums of all time, the record garnered a lot of interest because many songs were rumoured to be about her ex-beau Harry Styles.

Her record-breaking album dovetailed into a record-breaking tour. 'The 1989 World Tour' ran from May to December 2015, spanning multiple legs across Asia, North America, Europe, and Oceania and setting new records for concert attendance and revenue. It grossed over $250 million in ticket sales worldwide, making it one of the highest-grossing concert tours of that year and then the entire decade. Many of the shows featured special guests including members of her 'squad' of girlfriends, plus other musicians and even sports stars.

Her retreat from the spotlight in 2016 gave Taylor her first break from the music industry in 10 years. Although the public backlash and continual scrutiny she had experienced was hard to take, it wasn't the only factor behind Taylor's hiatus. She had begun a serious relationship with British actor Joe Alwyn and had secretly moved to London to be with him.

As in typical Taylor fashion, she didn't just sit and relax during her off time... instead she focussed on writing a new album to re-set herself, taking inspiration from her tempestuous relationship with the media and the personal difficulties involved in navigating a love life against such a background.

The result was *Reputation,* released in November 2017. It was the first music fans had heard from her in three years and to say they were excited is an understatement. As Taylor ditched her innocent and intensely romantic narratives in favour of darker themes around fame, reputation and relationships, her songs referenced alcohol and sex and included swearing for the first time. A new sound called for a new aesthetic to go along with it. Dark and edgy ensembles were the vibe for Reputation. Everything had a hint of rockstar glamour, often featuring leather, studs, and dramatic makeup. Serpentine jewellery cast an aura of mystique and power over her look. She said the hit TV show Game of Thrones had also influenced her creative process.

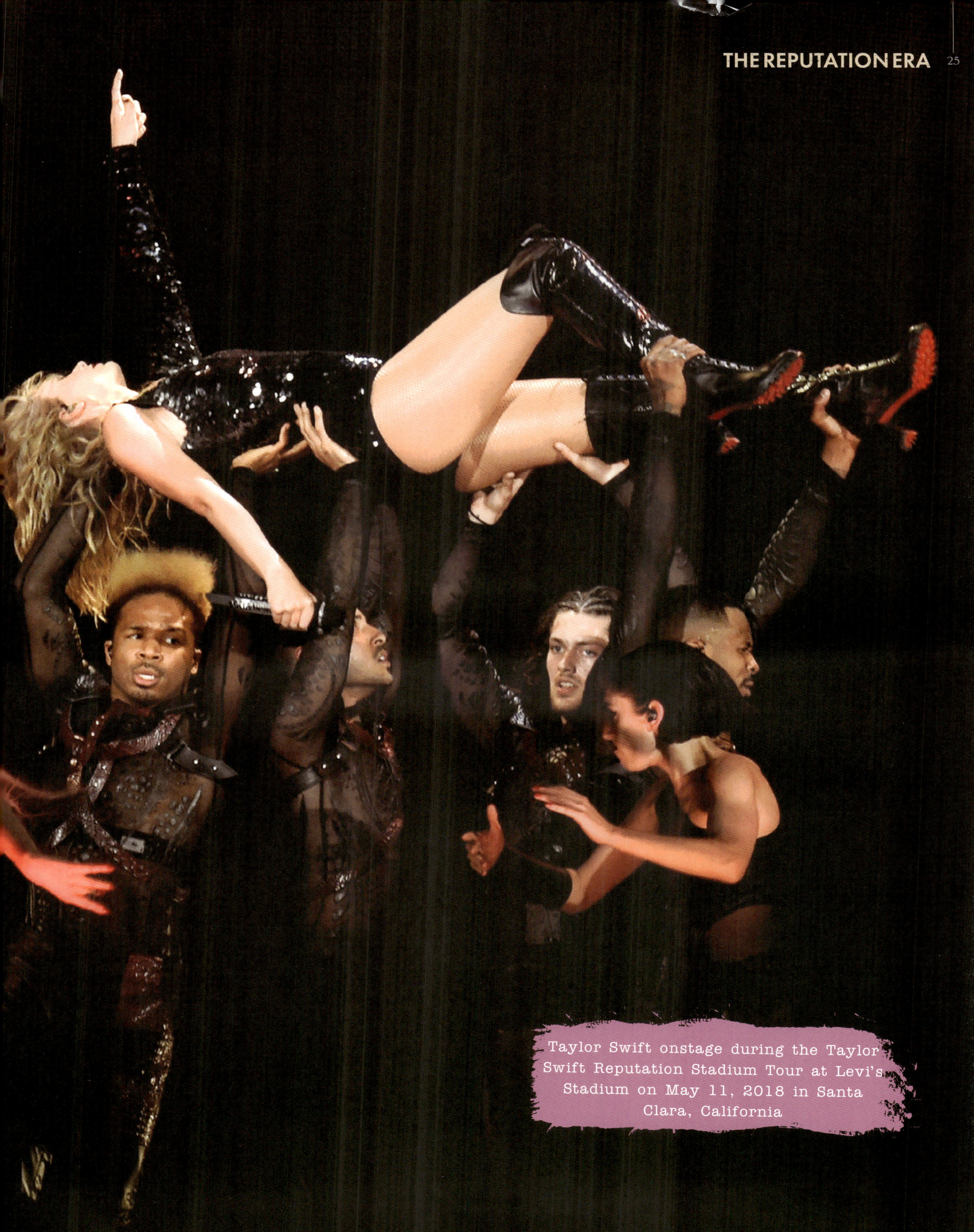

Taylor Swift onstage during the Taylor Swift Reputation Stadium Tour at Levi's Stadium on May 11, 2018 in Santa Clara, California

In keeping with the mood of the album, Taylor did not do any press interviews to promote it. Nevertheless, it topped the charts for three weeks, becoming her fifth number one hit on the US Billboard Hot 100 and also gained the most plays on Spotify in a single day. Reputation became the top-selling US album of the year.

By the time her Reputation tour kicked off Taylor only had her own records to beat – which she did, topping the gross and attendance figures set by the 1989 tour in a series of 53 all-stadium shows which ran from May to November 2018.

Once again, she had set the bar stratospherically high. The only records and standards left to beat were her own.

Miss Americana

The 2020 Netflix documentary *Miss Americana*, showed Taylor's disappointment on hearing that Reputation hadn't received any Grammy nominations. 'If I don't beat anything I've done prior, it's a failure,' she said, revealing the high standards she sets herself.

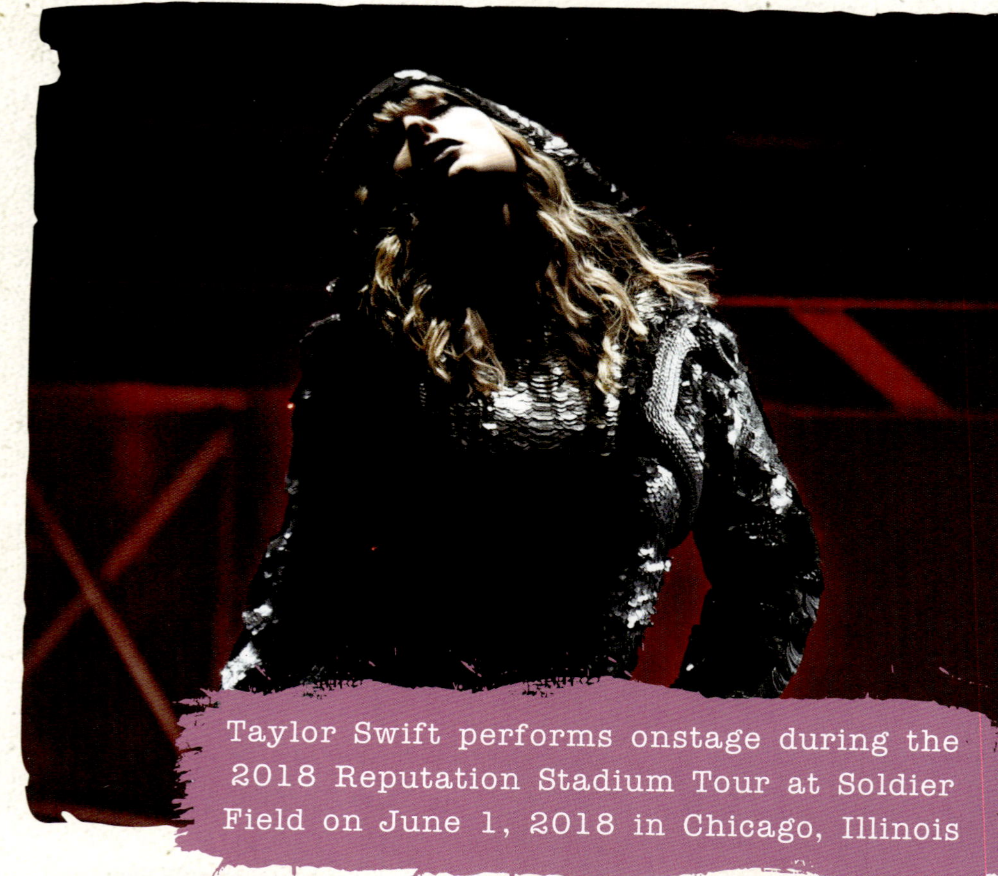

Taylor Swift performs onstage during the 2018 Reputation Stadium Tour at Soldier Field on June 1, 2018 in Chicago, Illinois

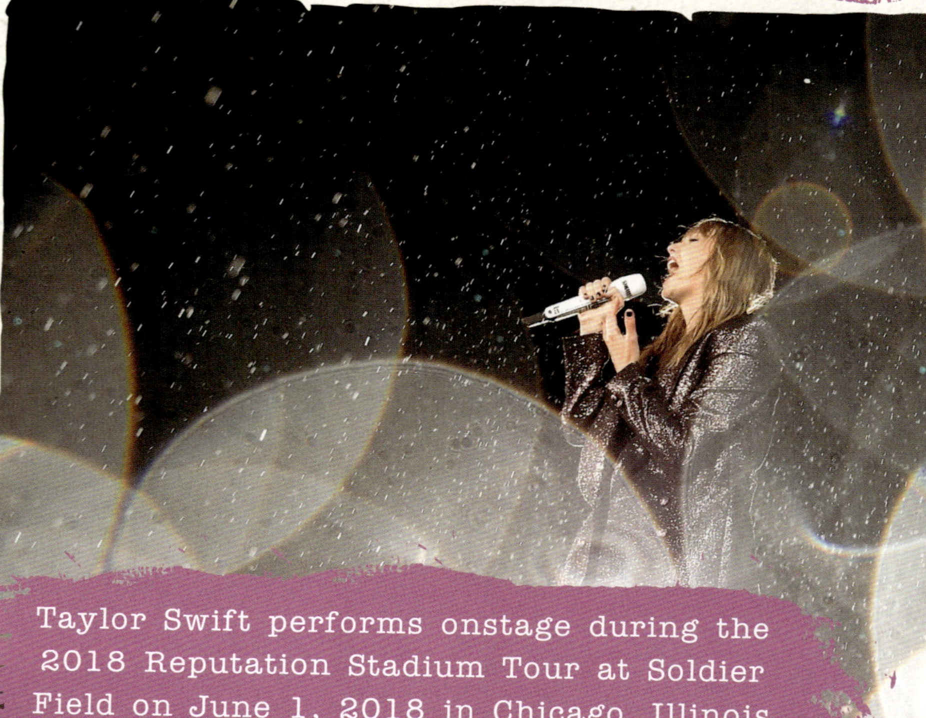

Taylor Swift performs onstage during the 2018 Reputation Stadium Tour at Soldier Field on June 1, 2018 in Chicago, Illinois

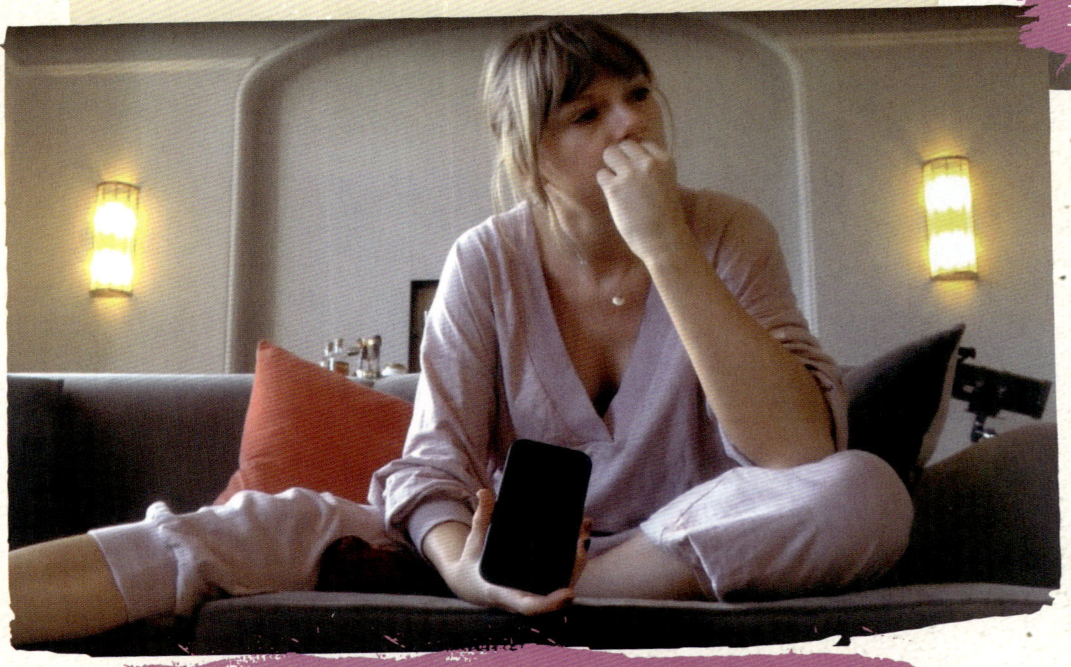

Still from the Netflix documentary Miss Americana, 2020

After 12 years her contract with Big Machine label had expired and in late 2018, she signed with Republic Records, part of the Universal Music Group. While it was undoubtedly a multi-million-dollar deal, Taylor made the move as much for her rights as the money. The new contract agreed that she would own her own masters going forward.

However, her first six albums would still be controlled by the Big Machine label –which would come to lead to 'trouble, trouble, trouble'…

Lover(s)

Calvin Harris

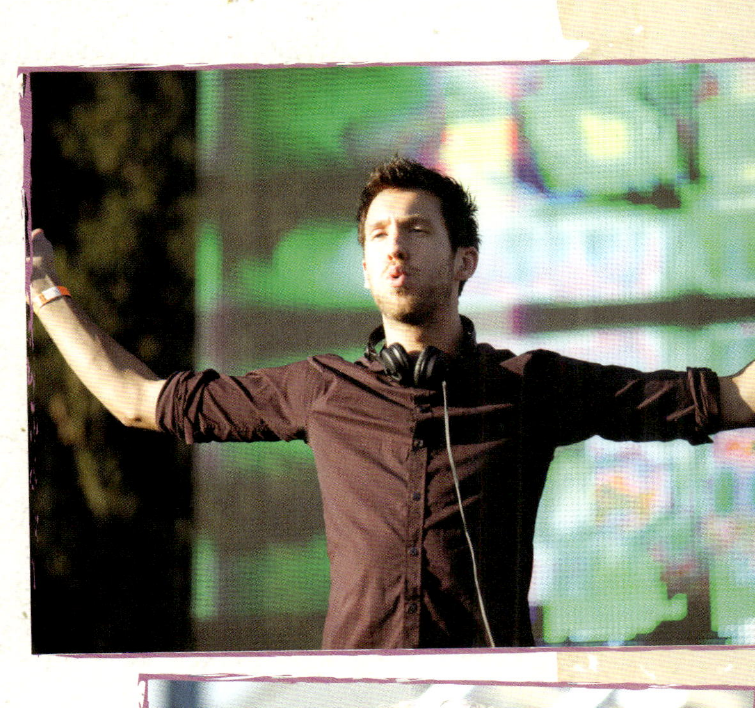

Swift and Scottish DJ Calvin Harris, real name Adam Wiles, dated for 15 months between 2015 and 2016, eventually breaking things off in March 2016.

In July, a spokesperson for Taylor informed People magazine that the singer had penned Harris' track, "This Is What You Came For," which featured Rihanna, using the alias Nils Sjoberg. This disclosure followed Harris' remarks in an interview where he expressed reluctance about collaborating with his then-partner.

Tom Hiddleston

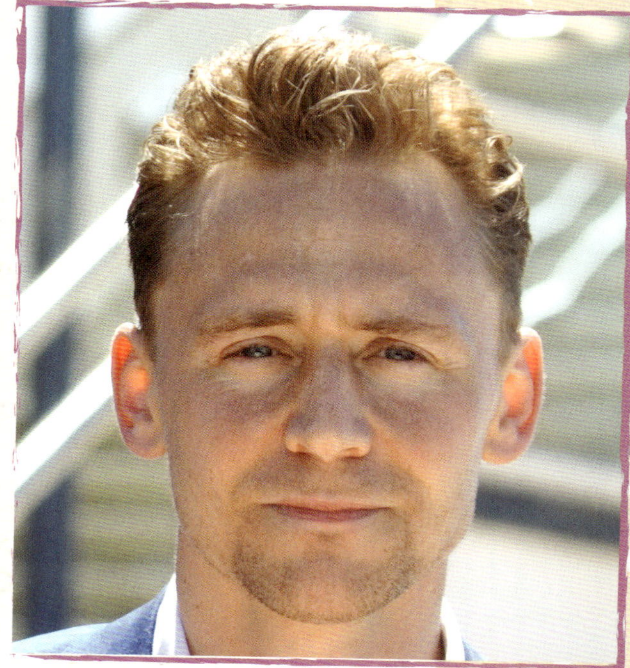

Swift had a short-lived romance with British actor Tom Hiddleston in the summer of 2016, following their initial sighting together at the Met Gala just days prior to Swift's split from Harris. Their relationship gained attention when they were photographed sharing a kiss on a beach in June 2016, and Hiddleston made headlines by donning his now-famous "I ❤ T.S." tank top at Swift's Fourth of July beach gathering.

Joe Alwyn

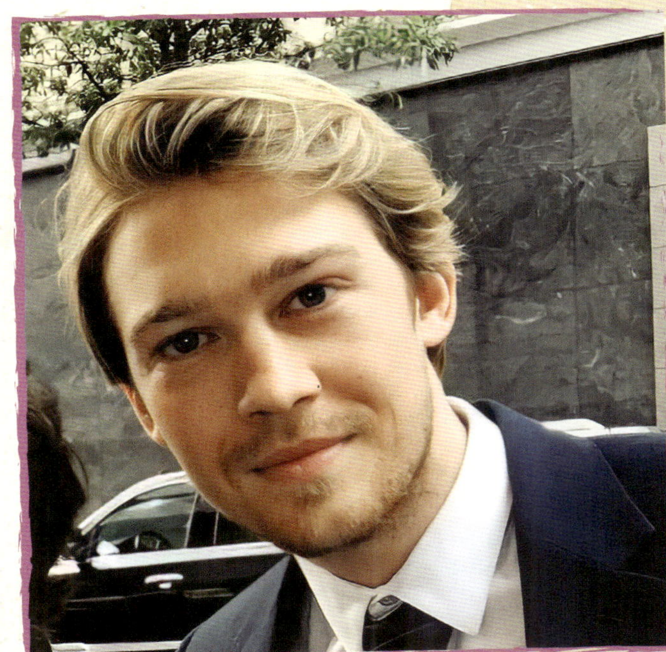

Taylor was rumoured to have met British actor Joe Alwyn at the 2016 Met Gala (while she was with Tom), a chance encounter that would result in a six-year relationship. It was Taylor's longest romantic relationship, spanning between September 2016 and April 2023. After months of travelling back and forth from the United States to England, the pair decided to move in together in London. Taylor and Joe spend the whole Covid 19 pandemic along one another's side, with commentators saying that they got closer than ever during that time when, as Taylor was also coping with her mother Andrea's ill health as she battled cancer.

THE LOVER ERA 2019

The Afterglow...

In June 2019, Taylor was deeply upset to discover that Big Machine was selling the master recordings of her first six albums. Despite her prior acceptance that Scott Borchetta, the label's owner, might eventually sell them, she was furious when the deal was finalized. The buyer turned out to be Scooter Braun, a talent manager with whom Taylor had a contentious history, feeling he had bullied her before. Taylor vehemently opposed the deal, claiming that Borchetta had ignored her previous attempts to acquire the master tapes herself. She alleged that both Borchetta and Braun were effectively controlling her against her wishes.

Determined to regain control, she embarked on the immense task of re-recording all six albums from her back catalogue. By re-recording her old music, Taylor hoped that her new versions, rather than the originals, would be used in future licensing deals and preferred by fans.

But in the meantime, she had a new album to promote. Her 2019 album *Lover* was the first that she would fully 'own'. Though Taylor described the upbeat album as 'a love letter to love itself', the lyrics are decidedly more political than any of her previous work. Taylor is now famous for her unwavering commitment to her values and her fearless stance against sexism and discrimination of all types but that hasn't always been the case. Despite sharing so much with her fans over the years, Taylor had chosen to keep quiet about her personal and political views. But no more.

She became a spokesperson for causes she believes in, such as feminism, LGBTQ+ rights, various other social justice issues and political engagement and activism.

Taylor Swift attends the InStyle and Warner Bros. Golden Globes After Party 2019 at The Beverly Hilton Hotel

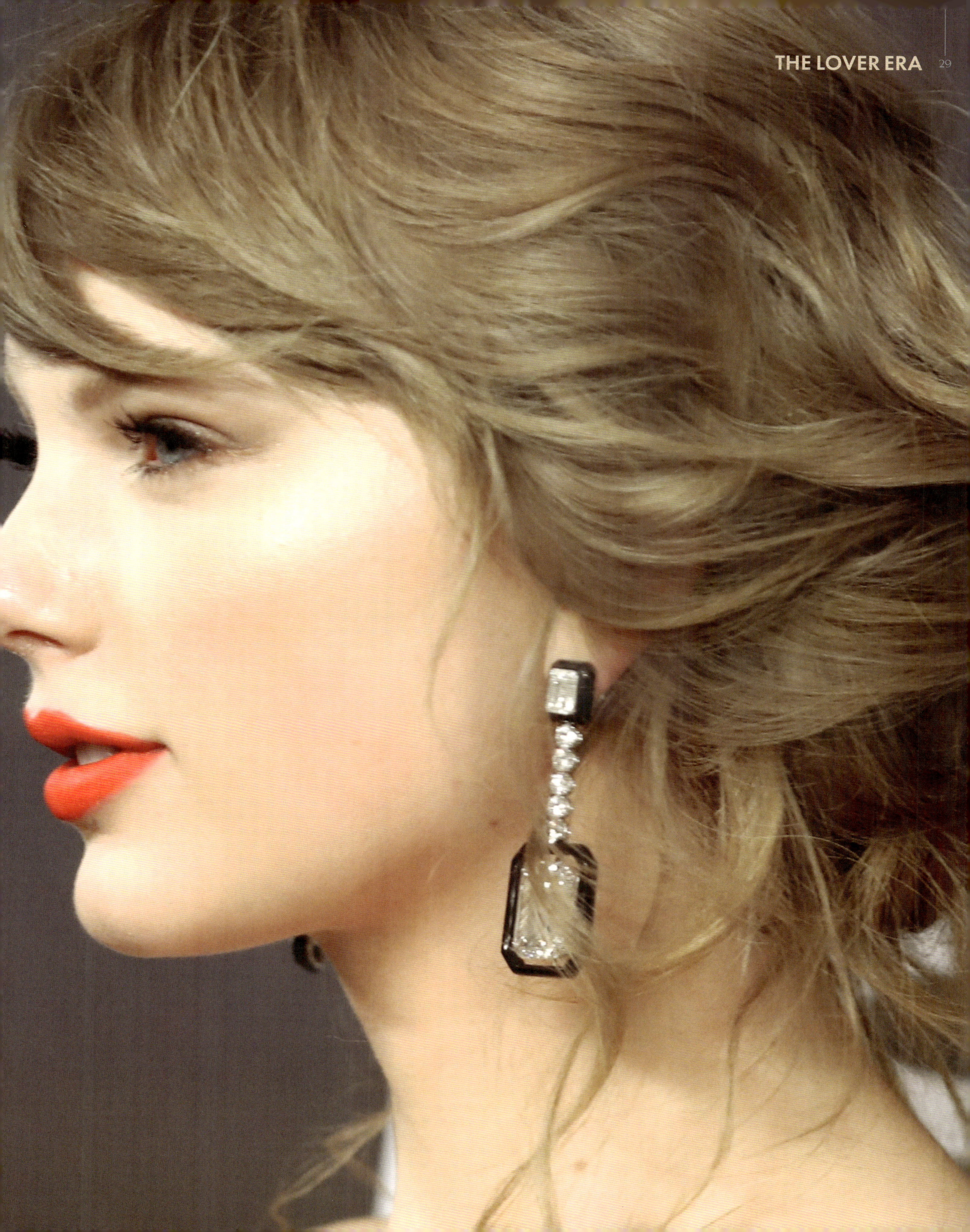

STELLAR SINGLE
The Man

As ever, Taylor has used music to expand on her thoughts and she highlighted the particular career challenges and barriers women face in her track *The Man*.

By imagining her life from a male perspective, Taylor uses this feminist anthem to address the idea that while men are praised for being assertive, ambitious, and dominant, women are often expected to be submissive and accommodating, grateful for their success and content not to strive for more.

Viewers of Taylor's Netflix documentary *Miss Americana* inferred that Taylor wrote this song immediately after hearing, in the opening scenes, that her album *Reputation* had not received any Grammy nominations.

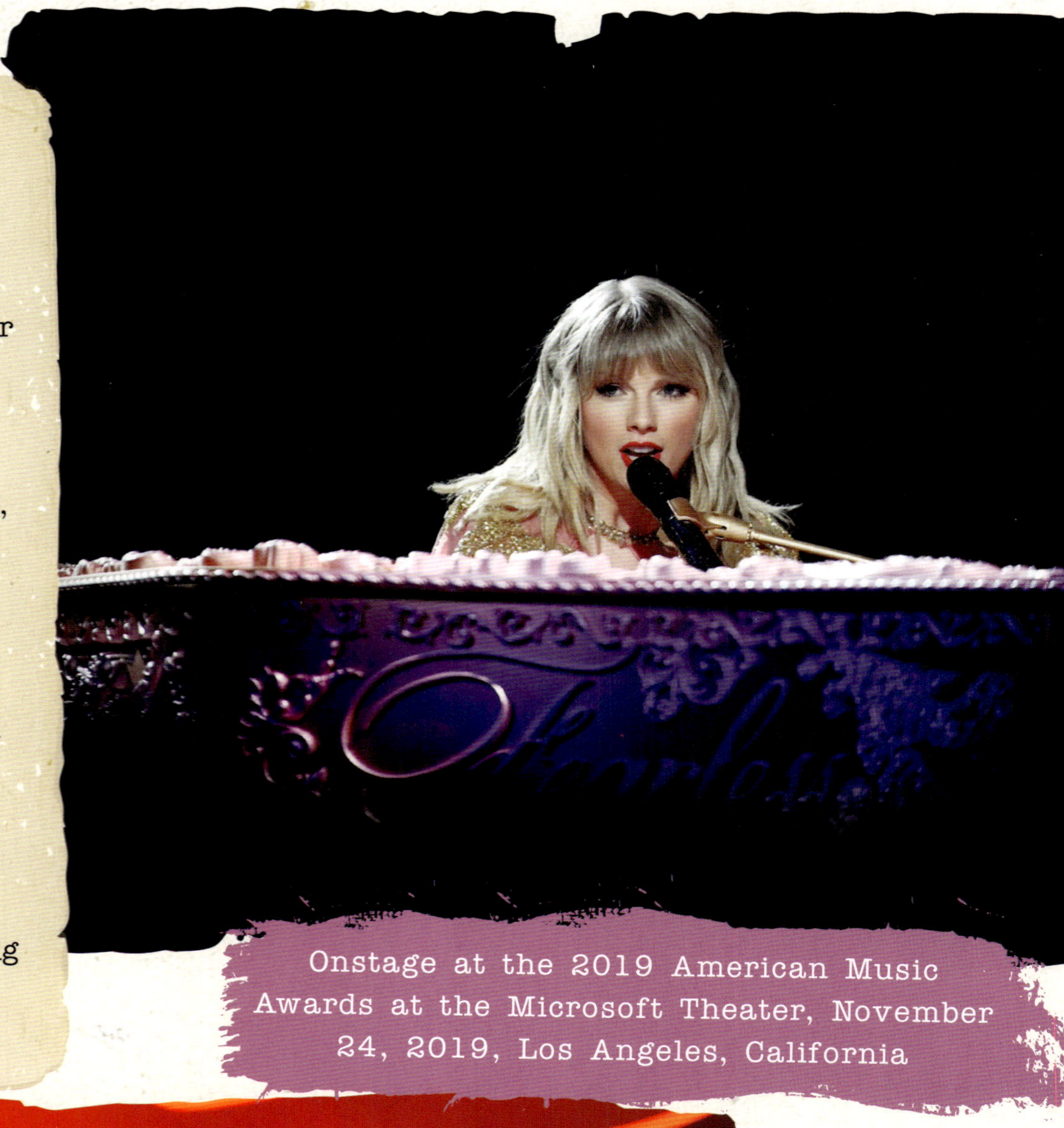

Onstage at the 2019 American Music Awards at the Microsoft Theater, November 24, 2019, Los Angeles, California

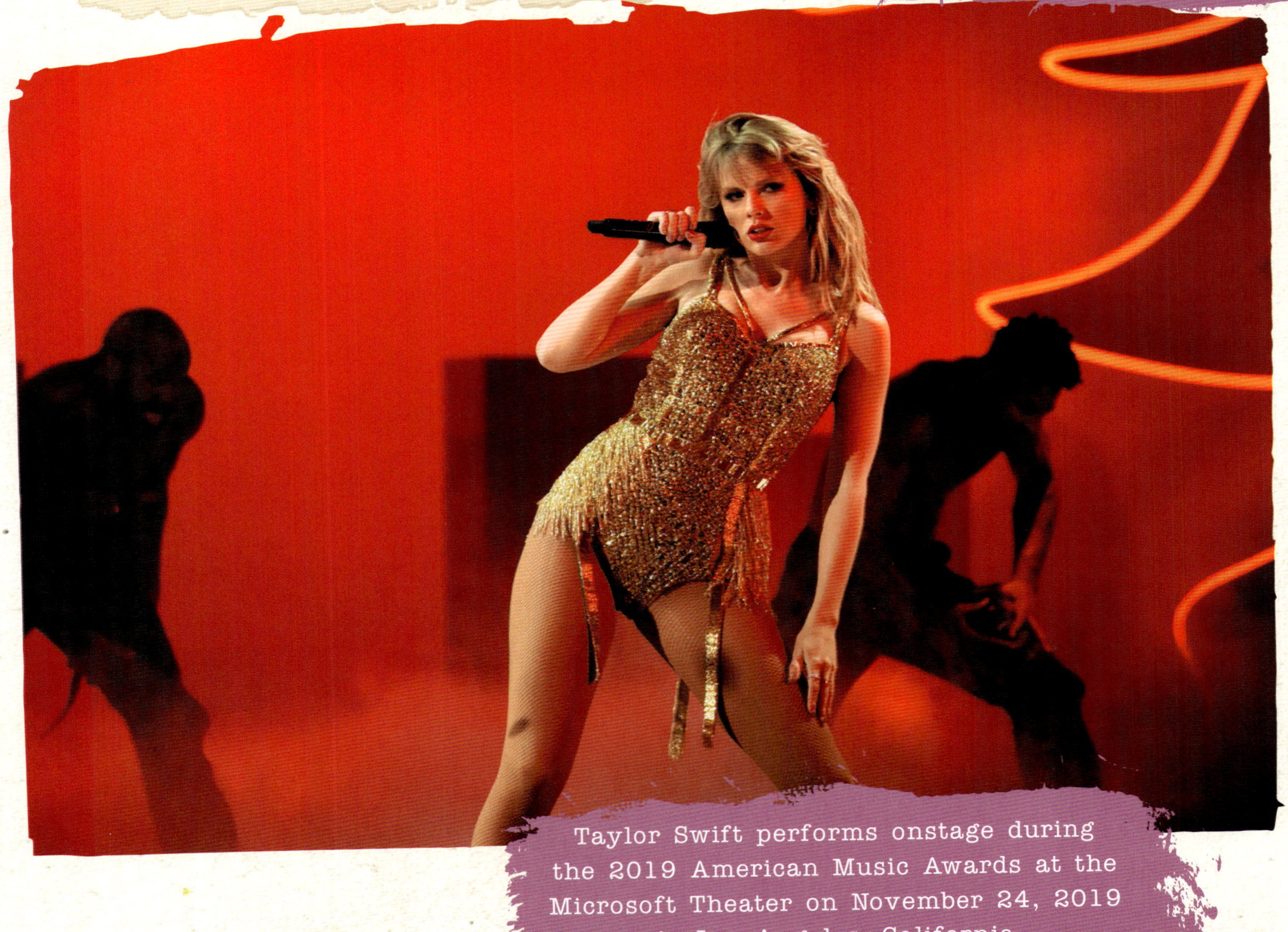

Taylor Swift performs onstage during the 2019 American Music Awards at the Microsoft Theater on November 24, 2019 in Los Angeles, California

Lover perfectly encapsulated '… all the captivating, spellbinding, maddening, devastating red, blue, gray, golden aspects of [love]'. This would be the last album she would release in her 20s and she took the opportunity to tap into her varied musical passions as she looked back over the first 30 years of her life.

Most critics reviewed *Lover* positively, praising its emotional honesty and free-spirited style. But plans to promote the album any further had to be cancelled because of the Covid-19 pandemic which put a stop to all festivals and concert tours in 2020, including Taylor's Lover Fest tour scheduled to begin on 5 April that year.

Forced to scrap her plans, Taylor had to stay at home like everyone else. But she used her time wisely, appearing to revel in the unexpected period of uninterrupted creative and writing time.

You Need to Calm Down

This track expressing her wholehearted support for the LGBTQ+ community saw Taylor leveraging her fame to encourage political action for the first time.

She was inspired to go public as a Democrat supporter by the 2020 Senate primary election in her home state of Tennessee.

She ended the accompanying video with a message asking her fans to support the Equality Act by signing her petition for Senate support of the measures. The video won Video of the Year at the MTV Video Music Awards and the song – also nominated for a Best Pop Solo Performance Grammy Awards – has since become very important in the LGBTQ+ community.

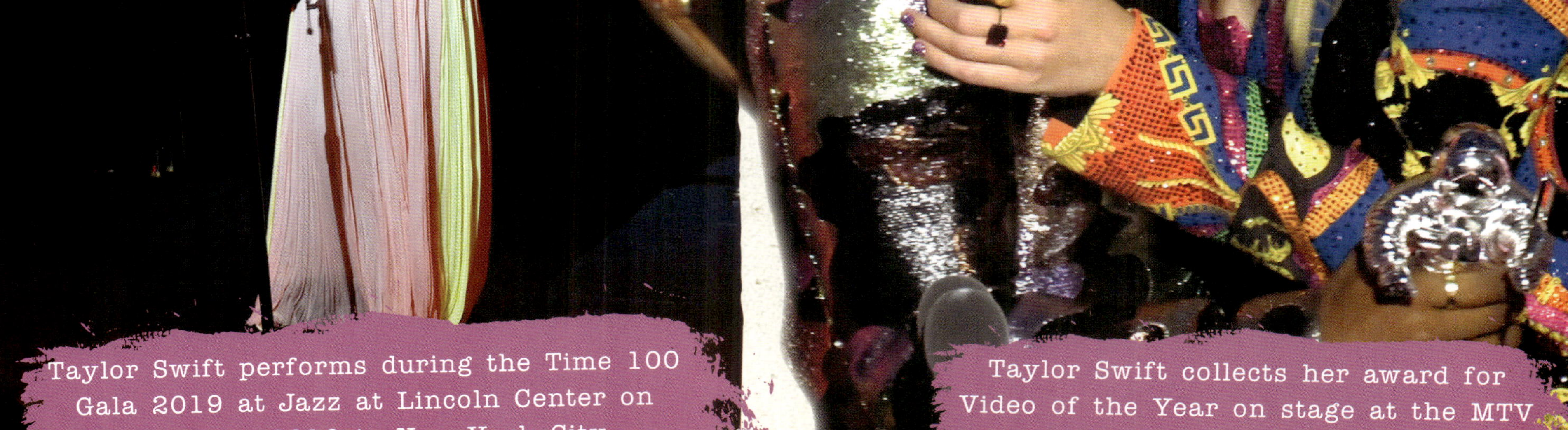

Taylor Swift performs during the Time 100 Gala 2019 at Jazz at Lincoln Center on April 23, 2019 in New York City

Taylor Swift collects her award for Video of the Year on stage at the MTV Video Music Awards 2019

THE FOLKLORE/ EVERMORE ERA

2020 Exile...

Fans were stunned when the surprise album *folklore* dropped in July 2020, completely out of the blue. With just a year passing since "Lover" and the Covid-19 lockdown still in full swing, no one anticipated new music from Taylor. Taylor herself admitted she hadn't planned for it either but found herself immersed in a rare period of uninterrupted creativity. She drew inspiration from the countless old films and classic books she indulged in during the early stages of quarantine.

The album consists of 17 fresh and truthful tracks, less showy than much of her previous, more pop-centred, output. In stark contrast to her previous work, Taylor plucked inspiration, not from her own experiences, but from her imagination. Now in a happy, long-term relationship with English actor Joe Alwyn she didn't have any real-life trauma to mine for content and so was able to avoid further media scrutiny by imagining characters and their emotions instead of using events from her own life.

In typical Taylor fashion, a new album and sound called for a new aesthetic. Folklore has a cottage-core style that romanticises escaping noisy modern life to return to simpler times. Lockdown vibes for sure. Quarantine chic was at the forefront in Folklore, as Taylor unveiled another new look featuring cosy and ethereal outfits with a folk-inspired vibe. Think knitted sweaters, flowy dresses, chunky boots and earthy tones.

Although Taylor kept her relationship with Joe very private, she has spoken about how their time together in lockdown meant that they began to write together, something that otherwise would probably not have happened. It's since been revealed that Joe has credits on Folklore under the pseudonym of William Bowery for the tracks *Betty* and *Exile*. Taylor even mentioned Joe in her Grammy acceptance speech, saying 'I had the best time writing songs with you in quarantine'.

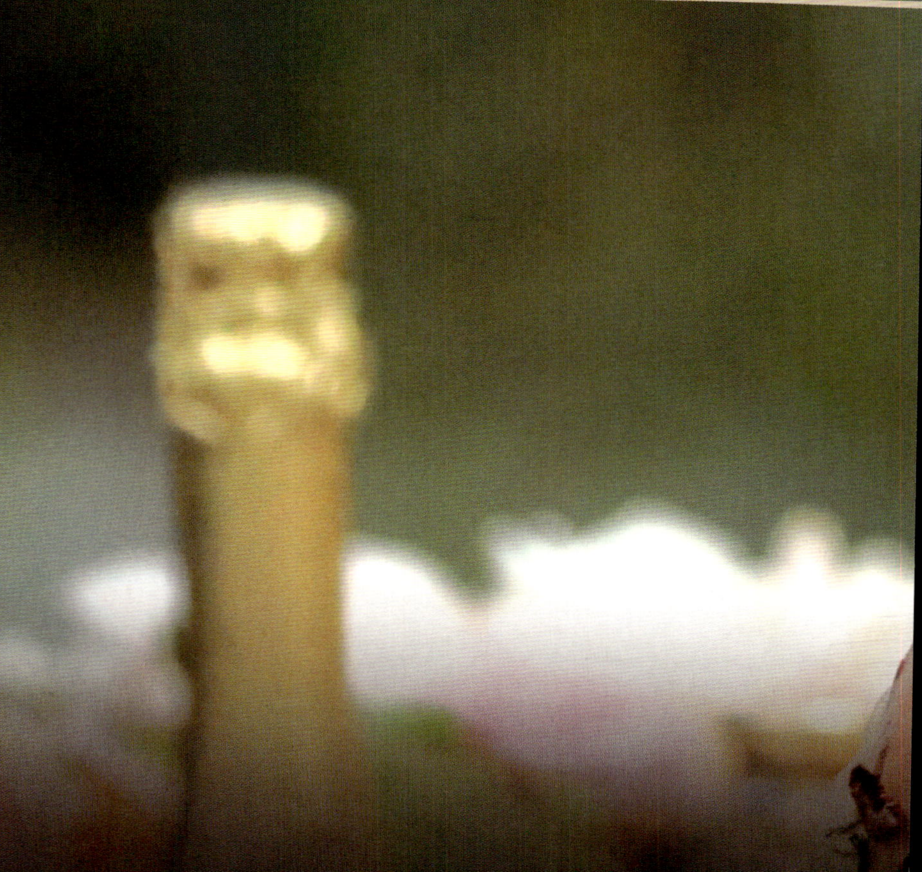

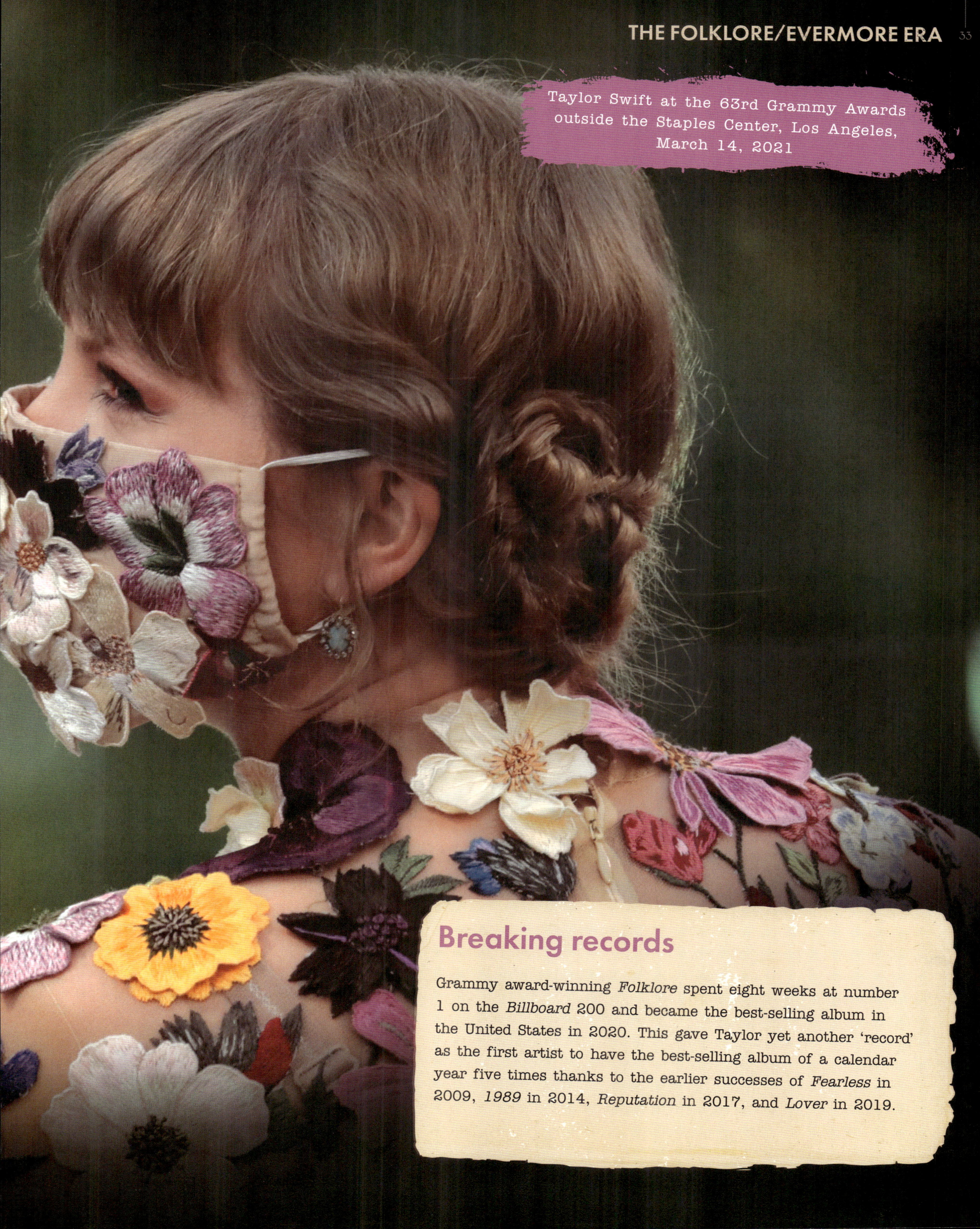

Breaking records

Grammy award-winning *Folklore* spent eight weeks at number 1 on the *Billboard* 200 and became the best-selling album in the United States in 2020. This gave Taylor yet another 'record' as the first artist to have the best-selling album of a calendar year five times thanks to the earlier successes of *Fearless* in 2009, *1989* in 2014, *Reputation* in 2017, and *Lover* in 2019.

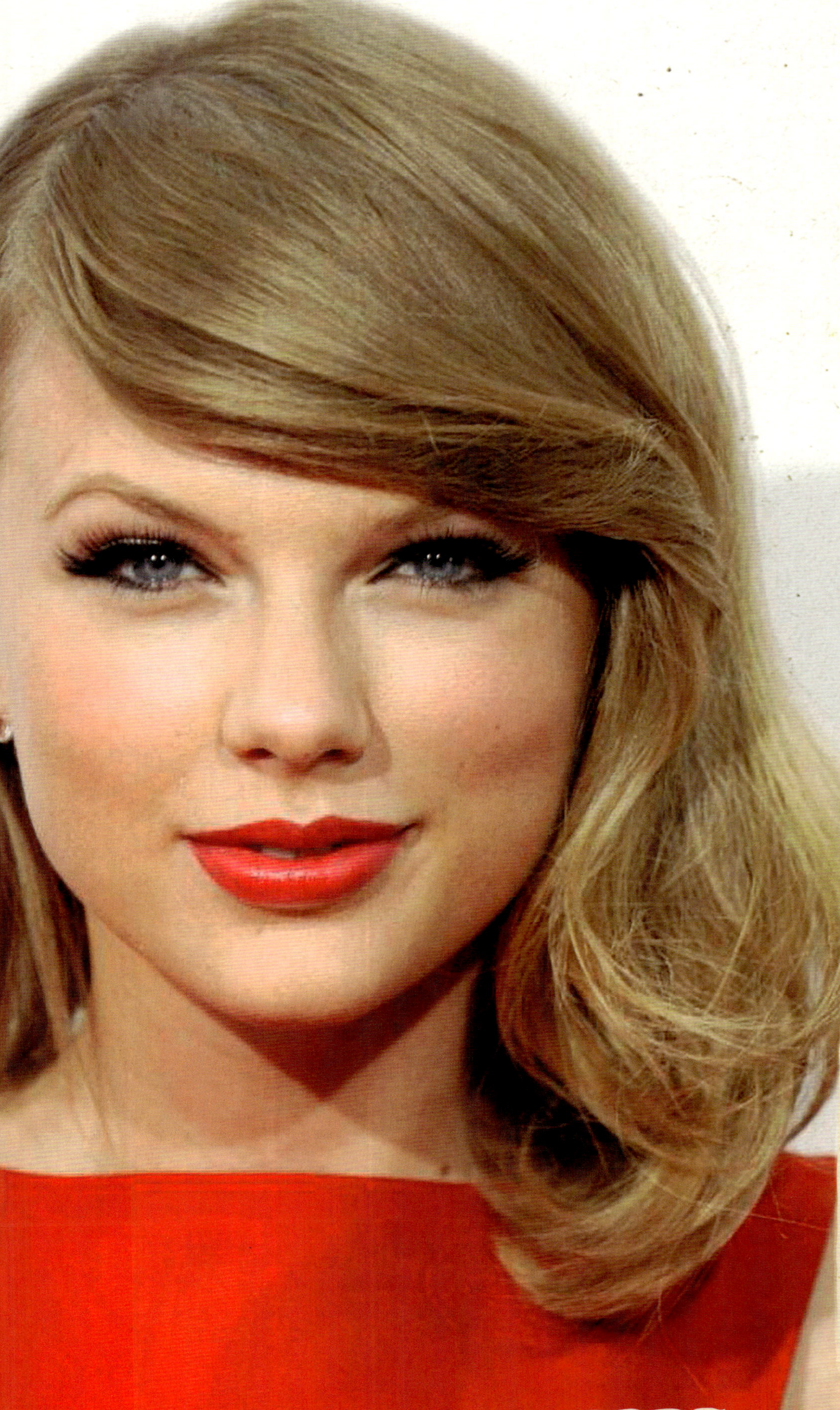

Taylor must have a taste for astonishing her fans as she surprised them again by releasing a second album, *Evermore*, described as a 'sister' to *Folklore*, only a few months later, on the 11th of December.

Like "Folklore," "Evermore" received praise for its intricate storytelling and was recognized as another introspective and restrained masterpiece. Once more, it drew inspiration from escapism and romanticism, delving into imaginary realms and fictional narratives.

Evermore was listed by various publications in their year-end rankings of the best albums of 2020 and received a nomination for Album of the Year at the 2022 Grammy awards.

'To put it plainly, we just couldn't stop writing songs," she told fans in an Instagram post.

STELLAR SINGLE
Cardigan

A song that stole the show when it came to its music video - *Cardigan* - released as the lead single from the album. *Cardigan* is the first of three songs connected in the story of what Taylor describes as a 'teenage love triangle'. All set at various times in the protagonists' lives, and telling of heartbreak, betrayal and yearning, the others are *August* and *Betty*.

STELLAR SINGLE
Willow

Willow is a lyrical love story, which became the third of Taylor's singles to debut at #1 on the Billboard Hot 100 chart, her seventh #1 in total and her second of 2020 following the success of *Cardigan*.

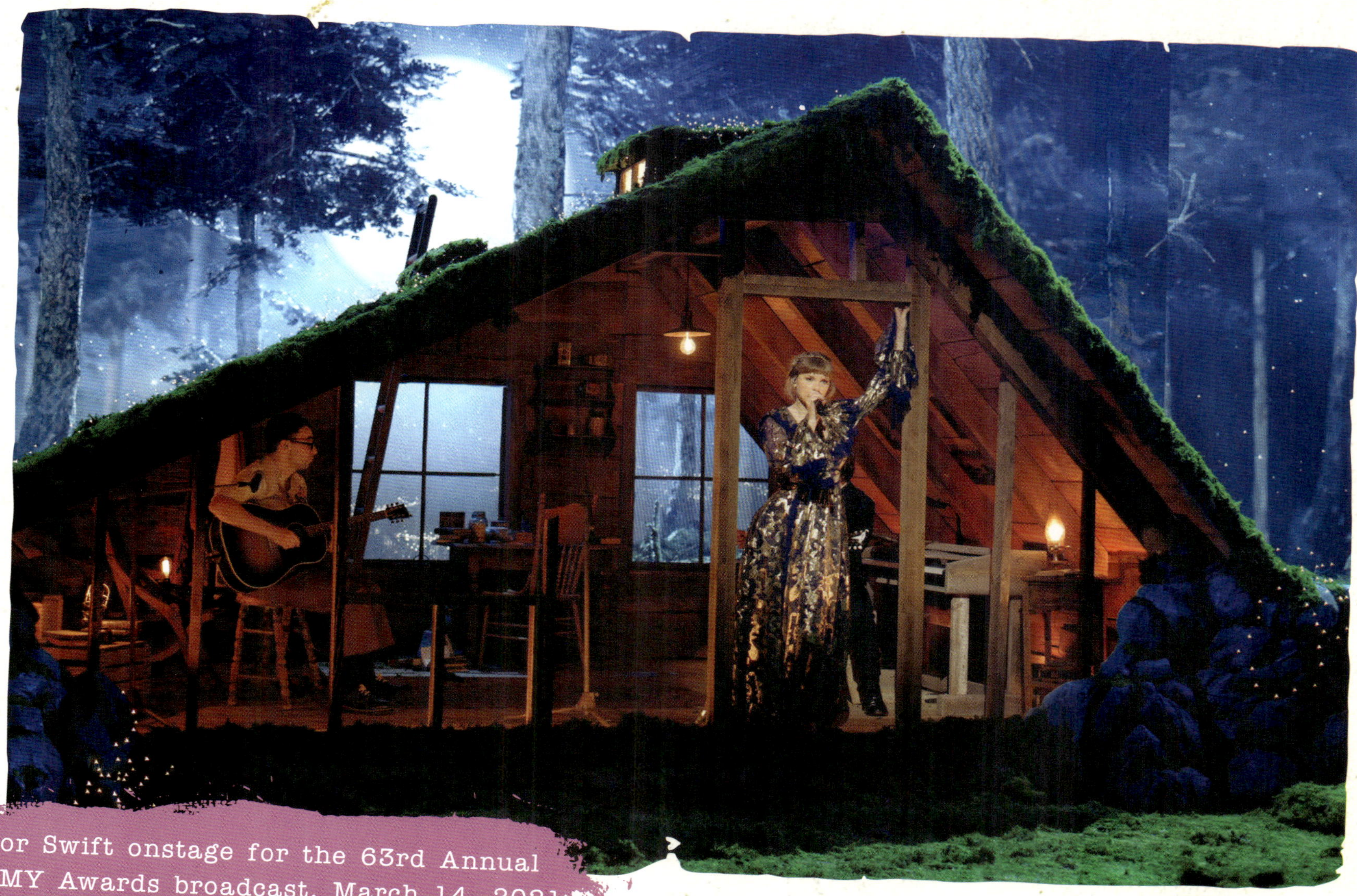

Taylor Swift onstage for the 63rd Annual GRAMMY Awards broadcast, March 14, 2021

Collaborators on this mesmerising album included Haim, members of The National and Marcus Mumford of Mumford & Sons. Justin Vernon from Bon Iver was back again but playing a bigger role than he'd performed on *Folklore*.

For the Evermore Era, Taylor enveloped herself in long-sleeved floral maxis and soft woollen coats and sweaters to layer a darker and more mysterious edge over the still cosy but more whimsical designs- a slightly more evolved rendition of her *Folklore* look.

Taylor dropped "Evermore" shortly before her 31st birthday, tweeting to fans that she was thrilled about this milestone because 31 was her lucky number backwards. She expressed that the album was a special gift from her to them, as a heartfelt thank you for their unwavering care, thoughtfulness, and support throughout all her birthdays.

Album of the Year for 'Folklore', during the 63rd Annual GRAMMY Awards, March 14, 2021 in Los Angeles, California

TAYLOR'S VERSION

Best thing that's ever been mine...

Despite releasing two brand new albums in 2020, Taylor immediately embarked on the monumental task of re-recording her first six albums she made while under Big Machine Record. By re-releasing her songs, Taylor ensured full ownership and creative control over her music. This bold endeavour not only served as a reclaiming of her artistic autonomy but also as a testament to her resilience and commitment to her craft.

Look what you made me do...

Fellow pop singer Kelly Clarkson recently spoke about how Taylor sends her a bouquet of flowers with every re-recorded album she releases.

This is because Kelly was the first person to publicly suggest that Swift re-record each of her six projects originally released under BMR, tweeting on 13th July 2019: "@taylorswift13 just a thought, U should go in & re-record all the songs that U don't own the masters on exactly how U did them but put brand new art & some kind of incentive so fans will no longer buy the old versions. I'd buy all of the new versions just to prove a point."

Alongside these re-recordings, Taylor delighted fans to a treasure trove of previously unreleased songs known as "vault tracks". "Vault tracks" are all the songs that from her past eras that never made it onto the original albums, but now are seeing the light of day.

Onstage during the 36th Annual Rock & Roll Hall Of Fame Induction Ceremony at Rocket Mortgage FieldHouse on October 30, 2021 in Cleveland, Ohio

After releasing the first two of her Taylor's Versions, Fearless and Red, in 2021, Taylor returned to new music.

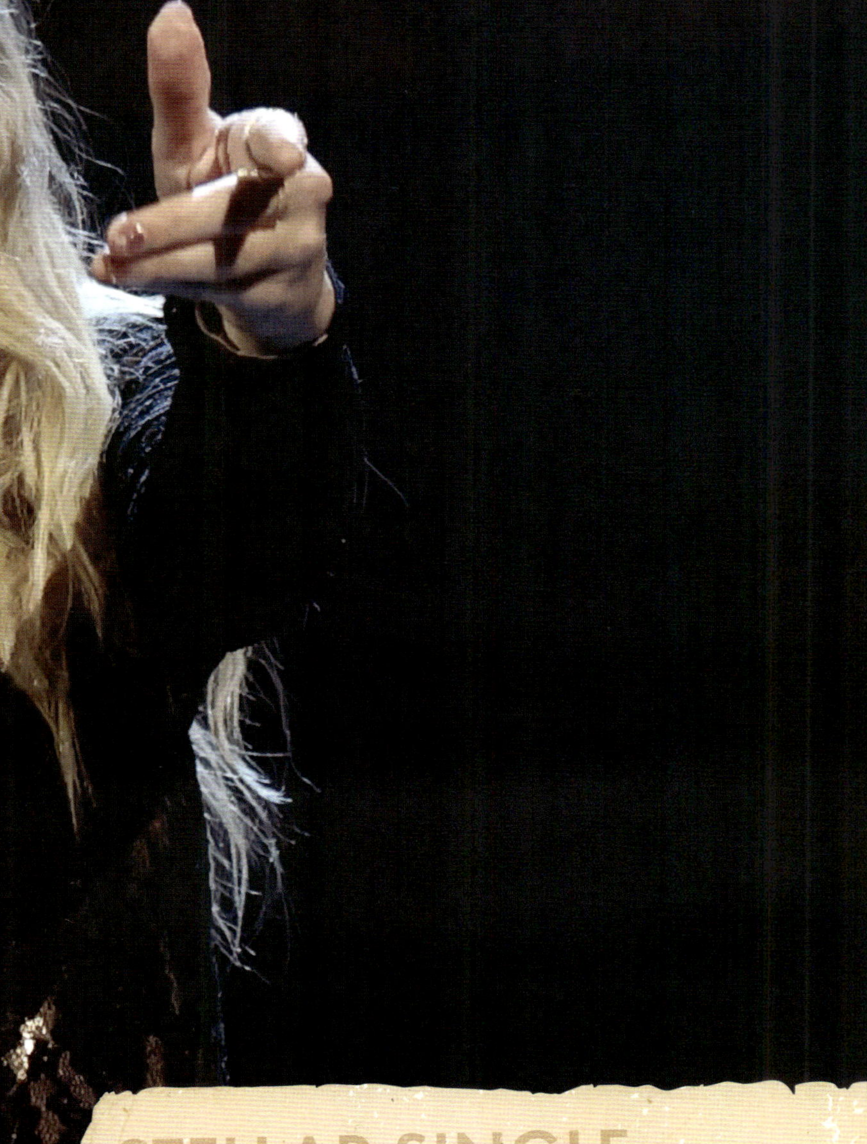

STELLAR SINGLE
All Too Well
(10-minute version)

Issued following the release of *Red – Taylor's Version*, this song, thought to be about Jake Gyllenhaal, was originally this long but cut back for the original album. Now released at its original length, it has gained cult status as the longest song to make #1 on the charts, beating the record held for 50 years by Don McLean's *American Pie* which was 8.42 minutes.

2021 - Fearless (Taylor's Version)
From the vault bonus tracks

You All Over Me
Mr. Perfectly Fine
We Were Happy
That's When
Don't You
Bye Bye Baby

2021 - Red (Taylor's Version)
From the vault bonus tracks

Better Man
Nothing New
Babe
Message in a Bottle
I Bet You Think About Me
Forever Winter
Run
The Very First Night
All Too Well (10 Minute Version)

2023 - Speak Now (Taylor's Version)
From the vault bonus tracks

Electric Touch
When Emma Falls in Love
I Can See You
Castles Crumbling
Foolish One
Timeless

2023 - 1989 (Taylor's Version)
From the vault bonus tracks

Is It Over Now? (Taylor's Version)
Now That We Don't Talk (Taylor's Version)
Say Don't Go (Taylor's Version)
Suburban Legends (Taylor's Version)
'Slut!' (Taylor's Version)
Sweeter Than Fiction' [Tangerine Vinyl Exclusive Only]

THE MIDNIGHTS ERA 2022

Meet me at Midnight...

In her last two albums Taylor experimented with a cast of fantasy characters so no one knew what to expect when she announced a new record was on the way.

Taylor reverted to a pop sound and autobiographical themes for her 10th studio album, "Midnights." Unlike her quarantine releases, this album was heavily promoted before its release, departing from the surprise-drop strategy.

Describing the album as a collection of stories from 13 sleepless nights scattered throughout her life, Taylor maintains a subdued and moody overall mood consistent with its title. As always, she presents herself both as a private individual and as her celebrity persona. 'It's a collection of music written in the middle of the night, a journey through terrors and sweet dreams," she explained. "The floors we pace and the demons we face. For all of us who have tossed and turned and decided to keep the lanterns lit and go searching – hoping that just maybe, when the clock strikes twelve... we'll meet ourselves.'

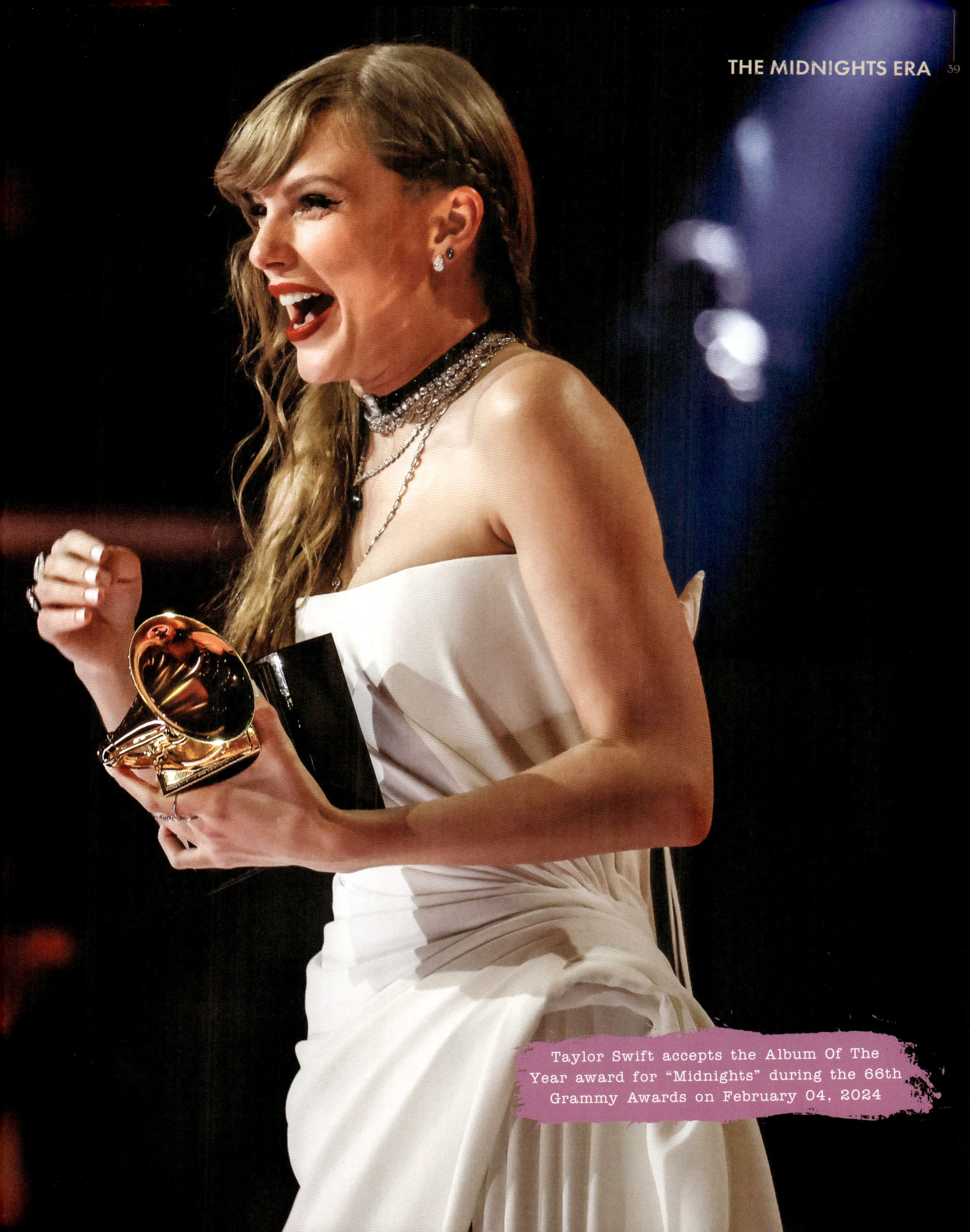

Taylor Swift accepts the Album Of The Year award for "Midnights" during the 66th Grammy Awards on February 04, 2024

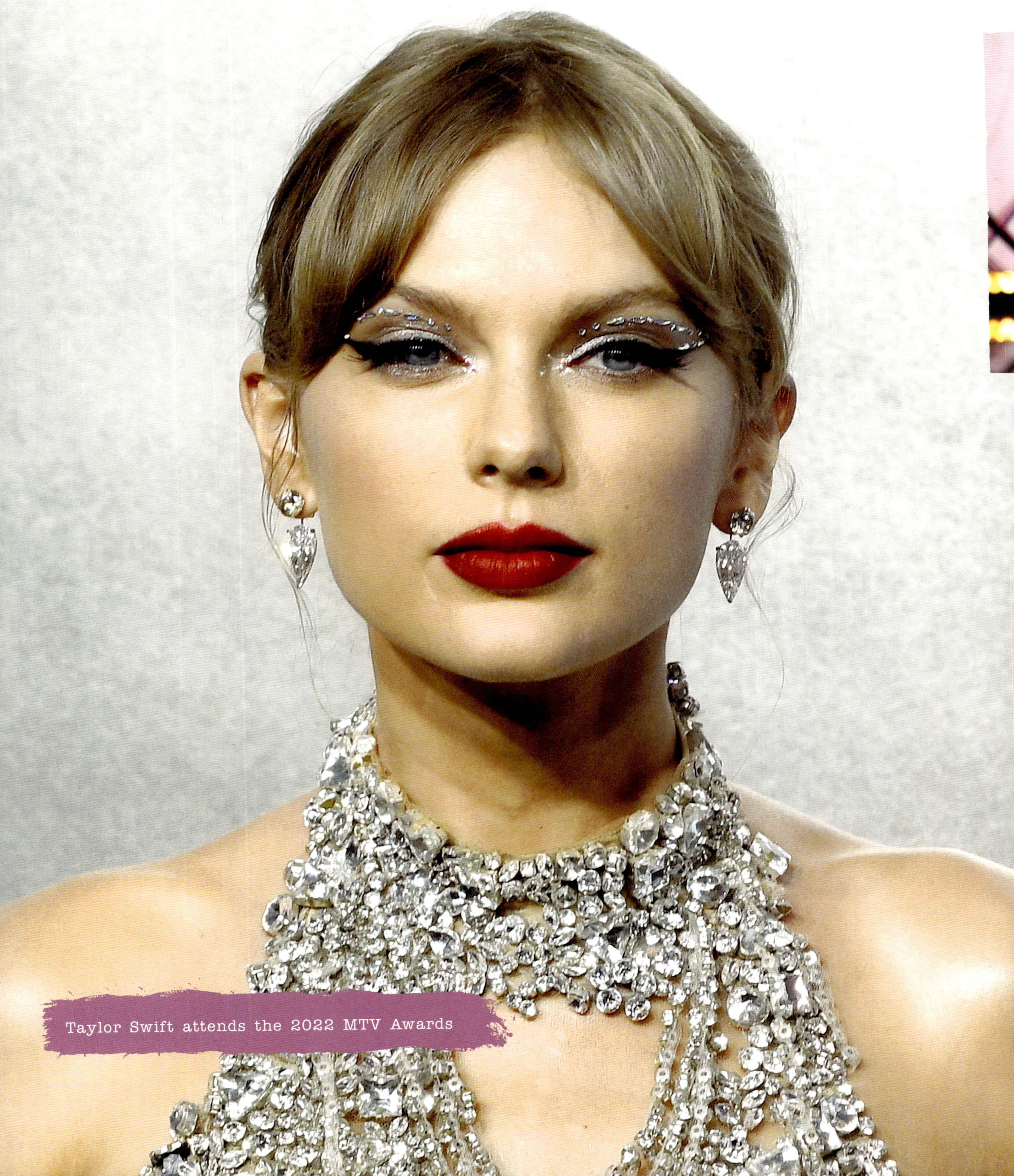

Taylor Swift attends the 2022 MTV Awards

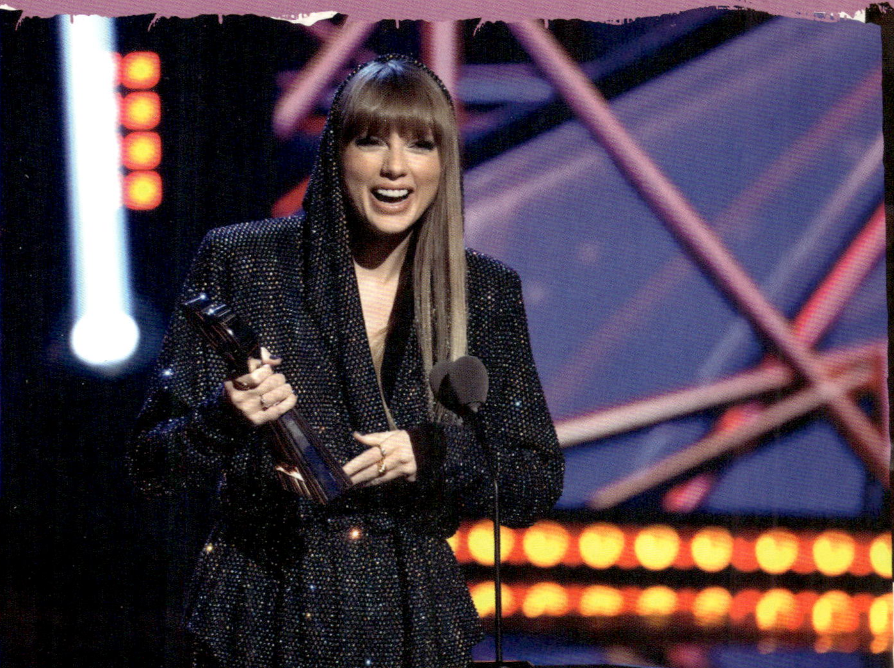

Taylor Swift accepts the Song of the Year award for "Anti-Hero" onstage during the 2023 iHeartRadio Music Awards

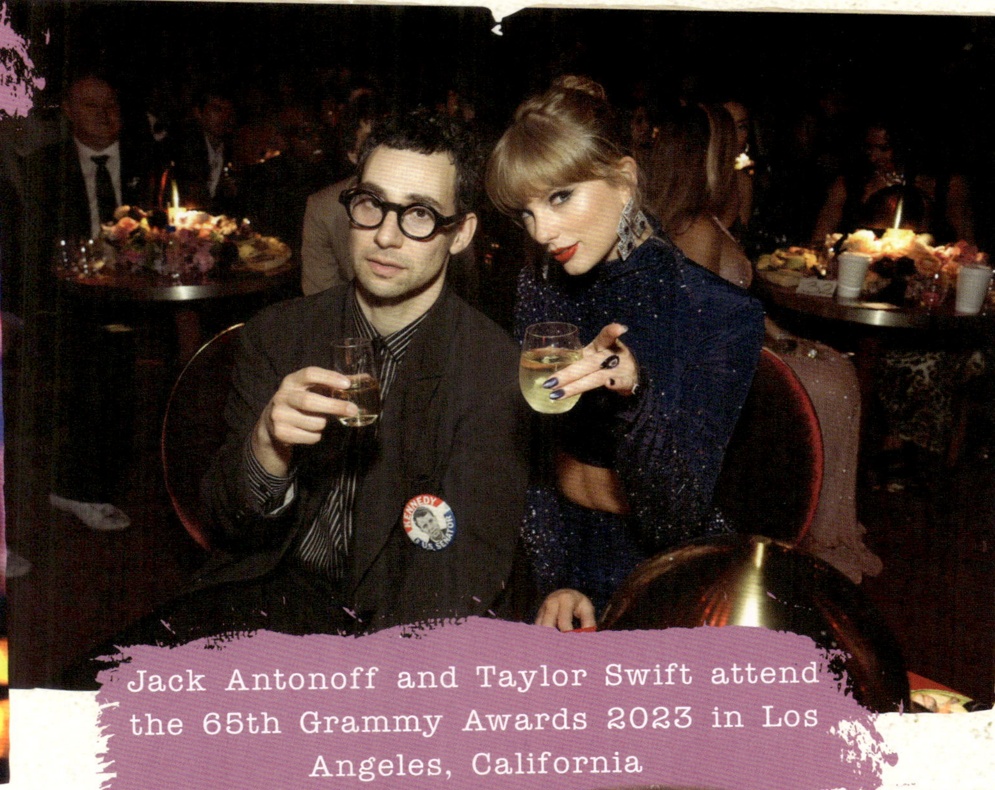

Jack Antonoff and Taylor Swift attend the 65th Grammy Awards 2023 in Los Angeles, California

Within 24 hours Midnights became the most-streamed album in a single day in Spotify's history, breaking the previous records, held by Taylor anyway, for *Red (Taylor's Version)* and *folklore*. The album also made Taylor the first artist in history to hold the top 10 spots on the Billboard Hot 100.

Three hours after the release of *Midnights*, Taylor surprised fans with the *Midnights (3 am Edition)*, including tracks which had been left out of the original album.

Taylor explained how she chose the extra, rather darker, 'vaults' tracks in an Instagram post, saying 'I think of Midnights as a complete concept album, with those 13 songs forming a full picture of the intensities of that mystifying, mad hour. However! There were other songs we wrote on our journey to find that magic 13. I'm calling them 3am tracks. Lately I've been loving the feeling of sharing more of our creative process with you, like we do with From the Vault tracks.'

Despite the serene tone of her recent releases, Taylor's workload has been anything but relaxed. With "Midnights" being her fifth album in three years and concurrently planning her blockbuster Eras tour, she's been kept exceptionally busy.

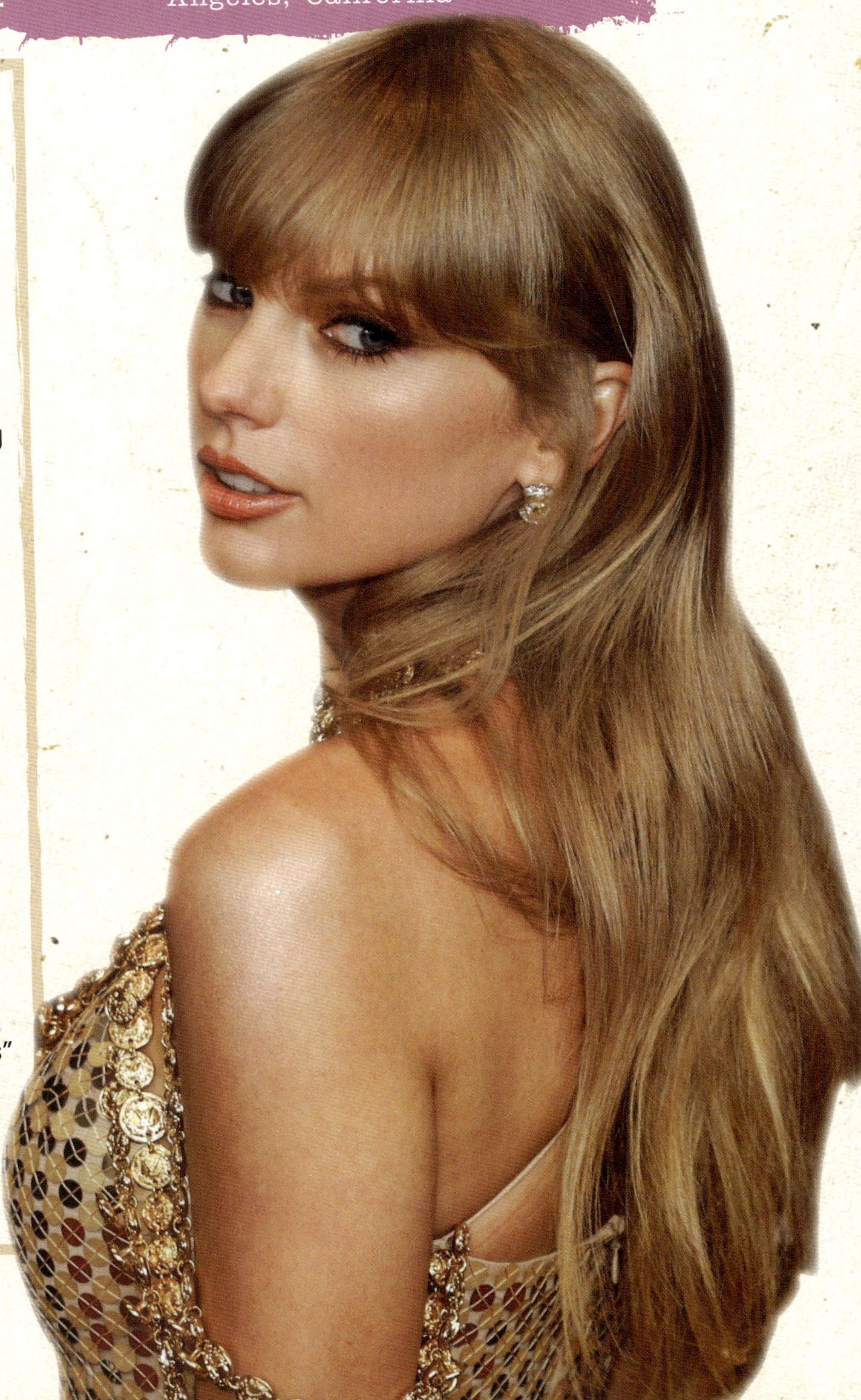

THE ERAS TOUR

Taylor's glorious, sell-out, record-breaking Eras concert tour has set the standard for bedazzling performance and state of the art production for years to come.

Her first tour in five years takes in 146 dates between opening in Glendale, Arizona, USA on 17 March 2023 and closing on 8 December 2024 in Vancouver, Canada, filling stadiums across five continents in between.

Demand for the sell-out tour was so fierce that websites crashed as fans clamoured for a seat. Concert industry experts *Pollstar* predict that the tour will gross US$1.4bn (£1.1bn) making it the highest earning tour by any artist, anywhere in the world – ever - beating the previous record set by Sir Elton John with his mammoth, farewell tour.

In a sweeping arc covering her entire career so far, Taylor performs 44+ songs, celebrating her 17-year, 10-album trajectory, in a show that runs well over three hours.

Taylor's spirited and wholehearted performance received widespread acclaim. Despite the show's length and intensity, as well as the complexity of being divided into 10 segments, each dedicated to a different album or era, Taylor never showed any signs of fatigue.

The only album without its dedicated 'era' and set list is her self-titled debut. However, on the opening night, Taylor surprised fans by including the hit single "Tim McGraw" from her debut album in the acoustic section of the performance, which changes with each show.

The segments, in sequence, include Lover, Fearless, Evermore, Reputation, Speak Now, Red, Folklore, 1989, Acoustic, and Midnights. With Taylor not having the opportunity to tour any music from Lover, Folklore, and Evermore due to Covid-19 restrictions, songs from these eras had their debut live performances, alongside a seven-song selection from Taylor's latest album, "Midnights," released in 2022.

In each section, Taylor recreates the aesthetic, feel, and fashion of the album's 'era'. So that's pastels for Lover, fringing for Fearless, dark cape for Evermore, snakes for Reputation – you get the idea – everything sparkling with crystals.

Taylor Swift during The Eras Tour at SoFi Stadium in Inglewood, California, Aug. 7 2023

Taylor and her fans: A Love Story

Taylor has one of most diehard and devoted fan bases on the planet. It's largely this profound personal and emotional connection with her fans that propelled her from mere superstar to a revered figure with almost cult-like status.

From her earliest days back in Nashville, Taylor has been famously accessible to her fans, the 'Swifties'. Understanding that many fans see her as being almost like an elder sister, Taylor has tried to stay as personally connected to them as possible. Despite her being a global phenom, Taylor has this amazing ability to remain relatable and make her fan base feel like they know her personally, and in many ways, they do because of how personal and honest her music is. Her fans become privy to even the most private moments of her life through her lyrics.

And let's talk about authenticity— which Taylor has in spades. There's no carefully curated content nor polished PR statements here. She's real, refreshingly candid, and unfiltered, sharing her thoughts on everything from politics to the latest pop culture craze.

At times it's like having a backstage pass to her life and creativity. She's all about sharing those juicy behind-the-scenes moments—whether she's in the recording studio, sharing videos when she's at home with her cats Meredith, Olivia, and Benjamin, or teasing us with sneak peeks of her latest music videos. It's like she's inviting fans into her world, showing us the real Taylor beyond the spotlight and the stage persona.

Taylor is all about keeping the conversation going with her fans. She doesn't just post and ghost—she's right there in the comments, showing her love and gratitude for their support. It's like she's building this community where everyone feels like they belong, and that's what keeps everyone coming back for more.

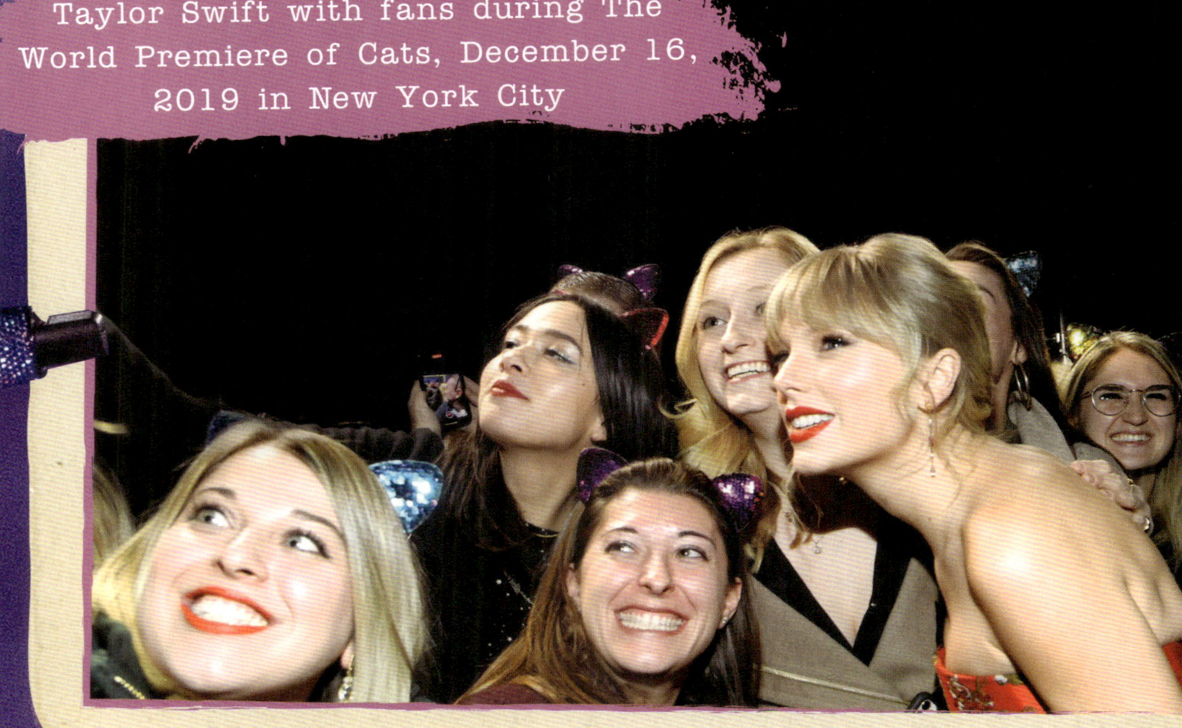

Taylor Swift with fans during The World Premiere of Cats, December 16, 2019 in New York City

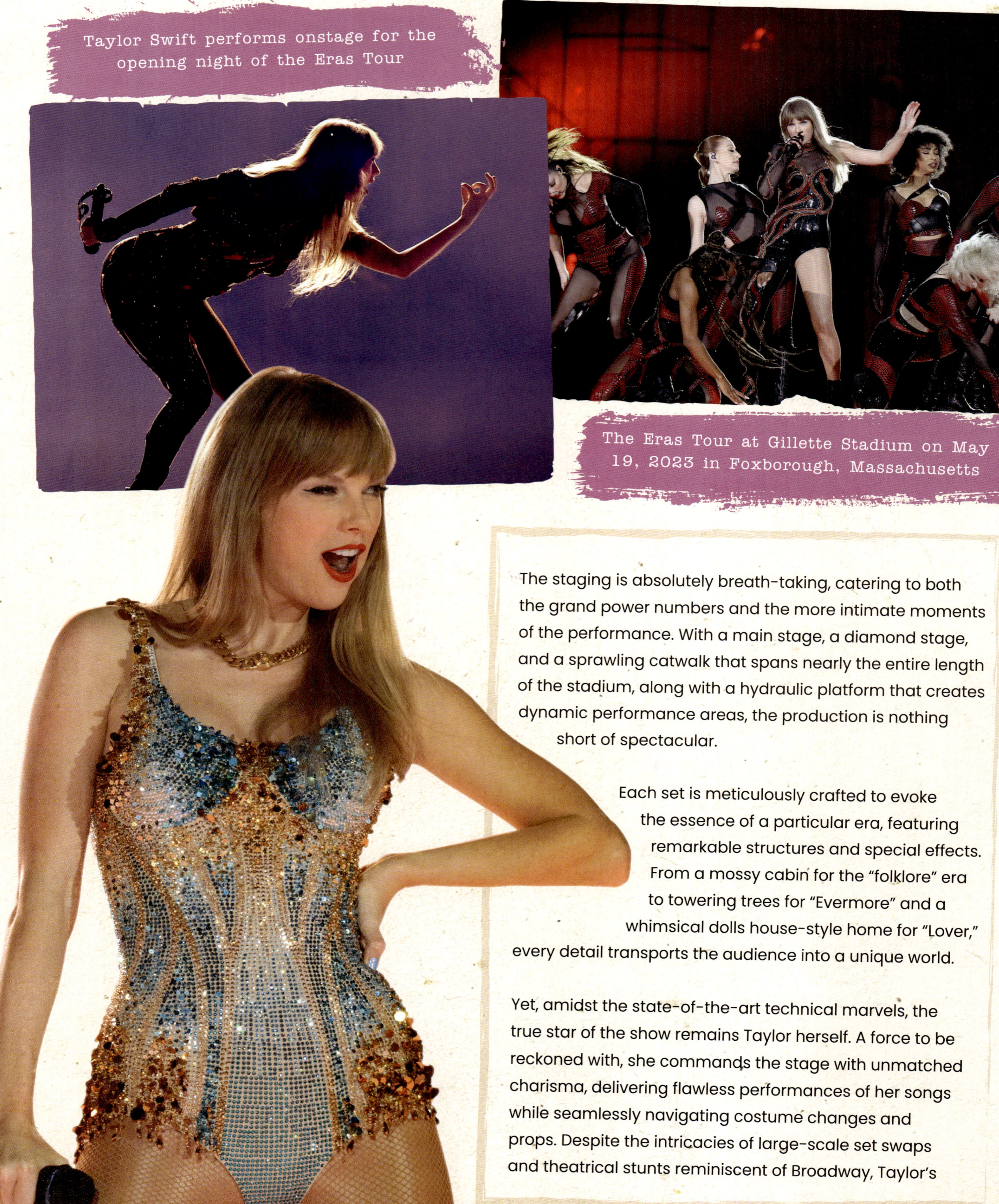

Taylor Swift performs onstage for the opening night of the Eras Tour

The Eras Tour at Gillette Stadium on May 19, 2023 in Foxborough, Massachusetts

The staging is absolutely breath-taking, catering to both the grand power numbers and the more intimate moments of the performance. With a main stage, a diamond stage, and a sprawling catwalk that spans nearly the entire length of the stadium, along with a hydraulic platform that creates dynamic performance areas, the production is nothing short of spectacular.

Each set is meticulously crafted to evoke the essence of a particular era, featuring remarkable structures and special effects. From a mossy cabin for the "folklore" era to towering trees for "Evermore" and a whimsical dolls house-style home for "Lover," every detail transports the audience into a unique world.

Yet, amidst the state-of-the-art technical marvels, the true star of the show remains Taylor herself. A force to be reckoned with, she commands the stage with unmatched charisma, delivering flawless performances of her songs while seamlessly navigating costume changes and props. Despite the intricacies of large-scale set swaps and theatrical stunts reminiscent of Broadway, Taylor's vocals remain pitch-perfect, showcasing her prowess as a performer.

She doesn't miss a beat or drop a note as she marches through pyrotechnics, smoke machines, and laser lights, belting out bangers. She then changes the mood entirely, highlighting her musicianship and stagecraft, as she croons a ballad and chats to the audience.

The 70,000-strong rapturous nightly audiences, predominantly female Swifties, lap it all up. They have to feel they had their money's worth as the show is in a league of its own.

All the while Taylor was performing on stage, putting on the most intricate and unforgettable shows for her fans, she was going through some personal turmoil of her own. After a six-year relationship, Taylor and Joe decide to go their separate ways.

To help get through her break up, Taylor turned to the thing she does best: writing songs. And just like that, 18 months after the release of Midnights, her heartbreak resulted in a brand new album called The Tortured Poets Department, released on the 19th of April.

ERAS CONCERT FILM

A recording of Taylor's Eras tour was released worldwide in over 100 countries on 13 October 2023, with advance ticket sales alone surpassing $100m (£82m).

Directed by Sam Wrench, the film, is advertised as a "breathtaking, cinematic view" of Taylor's latest tour. It was recorded over three nights from 3-5 August 2023 during a series of concerts at Sofi Stadium in Inglewood, California, USA.

2,200 Swifties were handpicked to join Taylor at the movie's premiere in Los Angeles on 11 October 2023.

'The capturing of the memories of this tour was so special because of what you brought to it,' Taylor told her fans. 'Your passion, your sense of humour, your attention to detail, the amount that you prepared for it, the amount that you cared for it. That is what I hope you get from this – how much you brought this tour to life.'

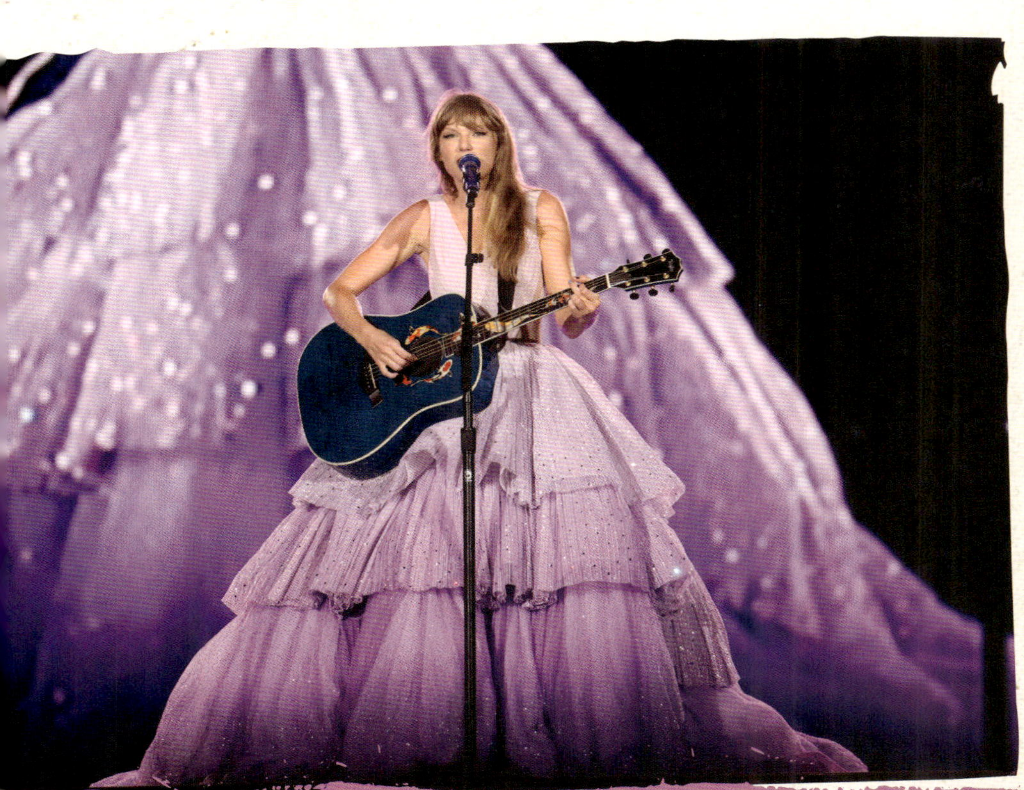
Taylor Swift performs onstage at GEHA Field at Arrowhead Stadium on July 07, 2023 in Kansas City, Missouri

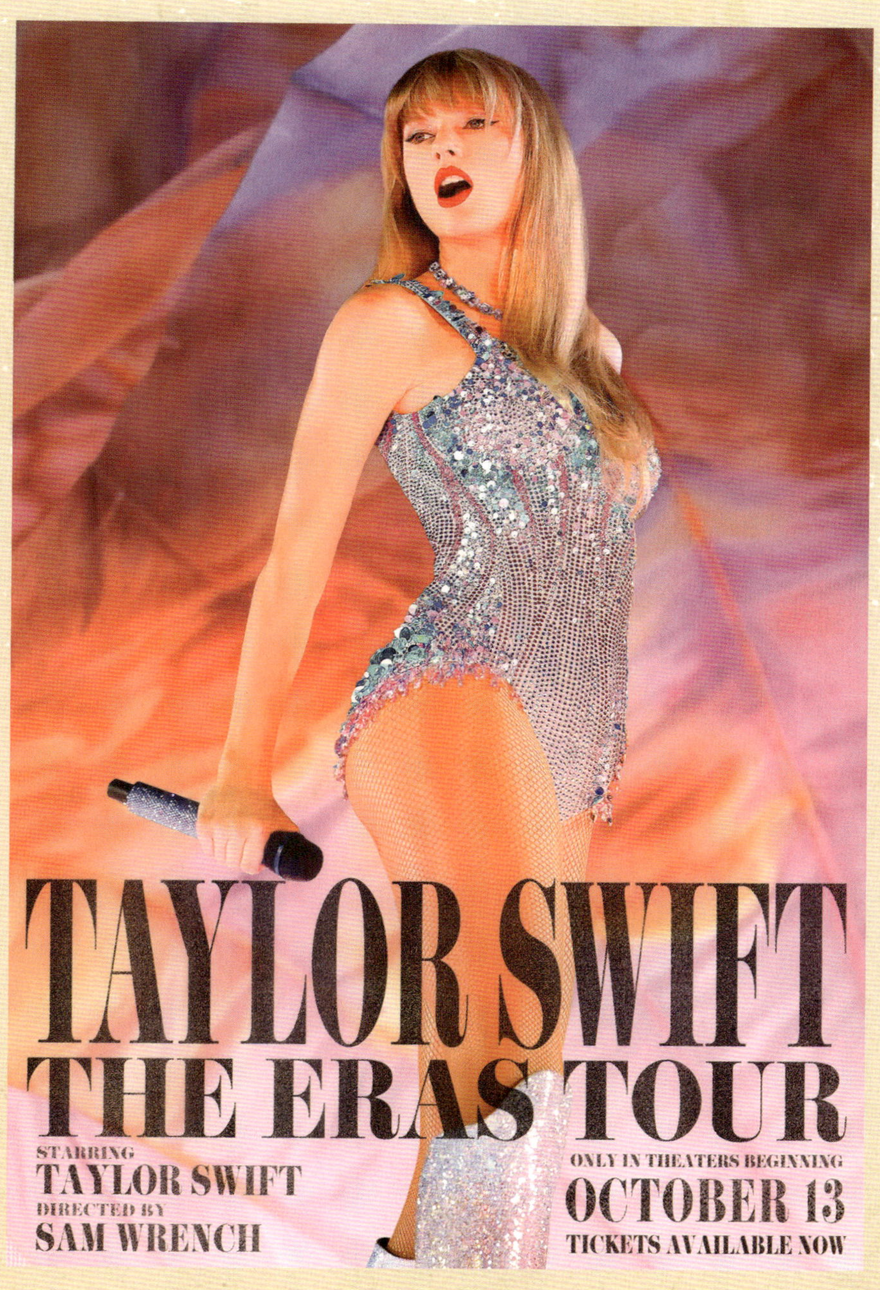

THE TORTURED POETS DEPARTMENT ERA

2024 I Can Do it With a Broken Heart...

As the news broke that her highly private six-year relationship to Joe Alwyn had ended, Swifties started Swiftie-ing, quickly recirculating a clip on social media of Taylor a few weeks earlier, onstage during an early Eras show, in tears as she sang "champagne problems"—a song she and Joe wrote together. It was a reminder that, despite the superhero-like aura she now radiates, Taylor, at her peak, still hurts like the rest of us. And that's exactly what she explores in her new TTPD album.

Taylor announced her 11th studio album in early 2024—while accepting another Grammy, as one does. Given her penchant for surprise announcements, perhaps we shouldn't have been caught so off guard. A few weeks later to a crowd of 96,000 in Melbourne, Australia, she said of her new album "I needed to make it, I've never had an album where I've needed song writing more than I needed it on *Tortured Poets*."

She worked alongside her trusted collaborators Jack Antonoff and Aaron Dessner, and returned to the soft, comfortable, bed-like sonics of *Midnights*, although with noticeably higher stakes. *Tortured Poets* has the intimate story craft and lyricism of *Folklore* and *Evermore*, yet

instead of fictional characters, Taylor went back to her roots and poured her heart out into her most personal work to date. The TTPD is a deep exploration of everything Taylor has been feeling, a plunge through the inner turmoil and existential angst that often accompany matters of the heart.

Taylor Swift performs during The Eras Tour at the National Stadium on March 2, 2024 in Singapore

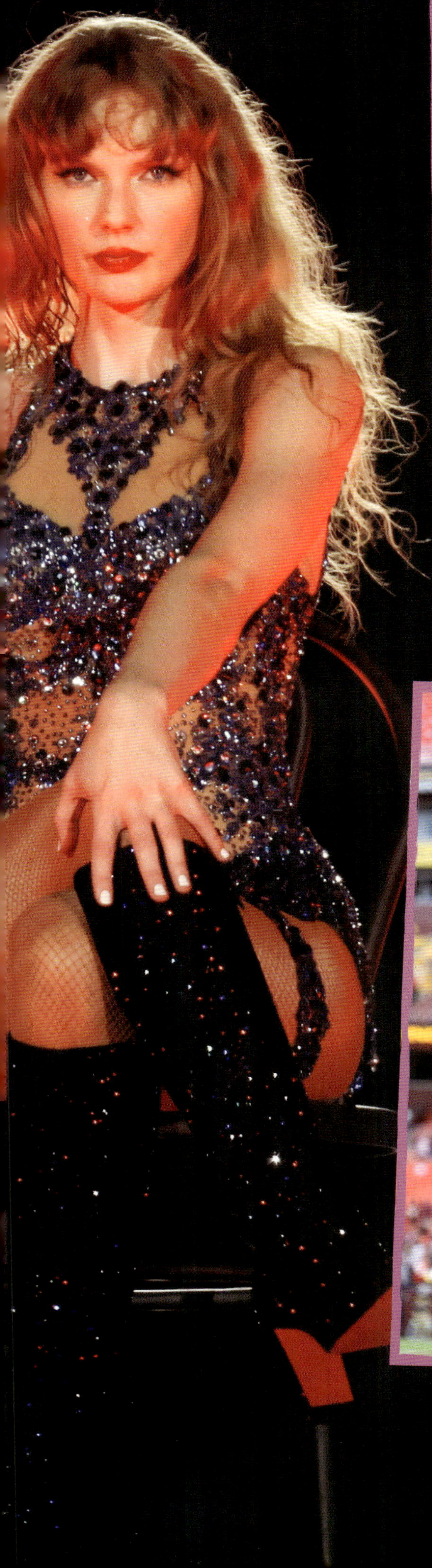

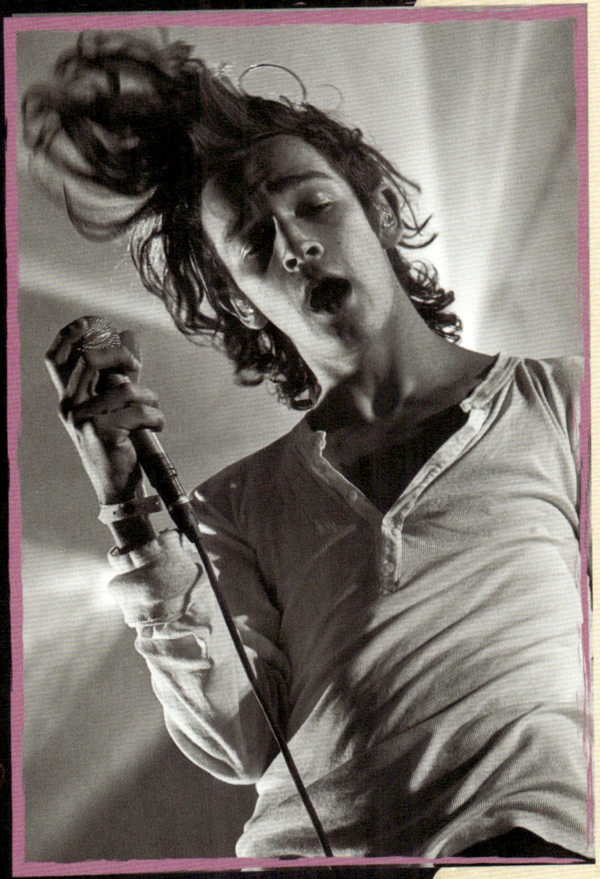

LOML

Matty Healy
May 2023 - June 2023
The Tortured Poet

This relationship goes all the way back to 2014, when Taylor and Matty first met. While the pair started out as friends, rumours swirled that Taylor was dating The 1975 frontman and in 2016, he made some not-so-friendly comments about the possibility of that happening.

Fast-forward to January 2023, Taylor makes a random surprise appearance at The 1975's show at the O2 Arena in London, where she performs "Anti-Hero" live for the first time.

In May 2023, more Matty dating rumours began circulating again as Taylor was fresh off her six-year relationship with Joe. Entertainment Tonight reported that the two had been set up by Taylor's producer and long-time friend Jack Antonoff.

Fans have been perplexed by her choice in Healy, given he has garnered controversy over the years as the front man for rock band The 1975.

The couple eventually called it quits after a month of dating.

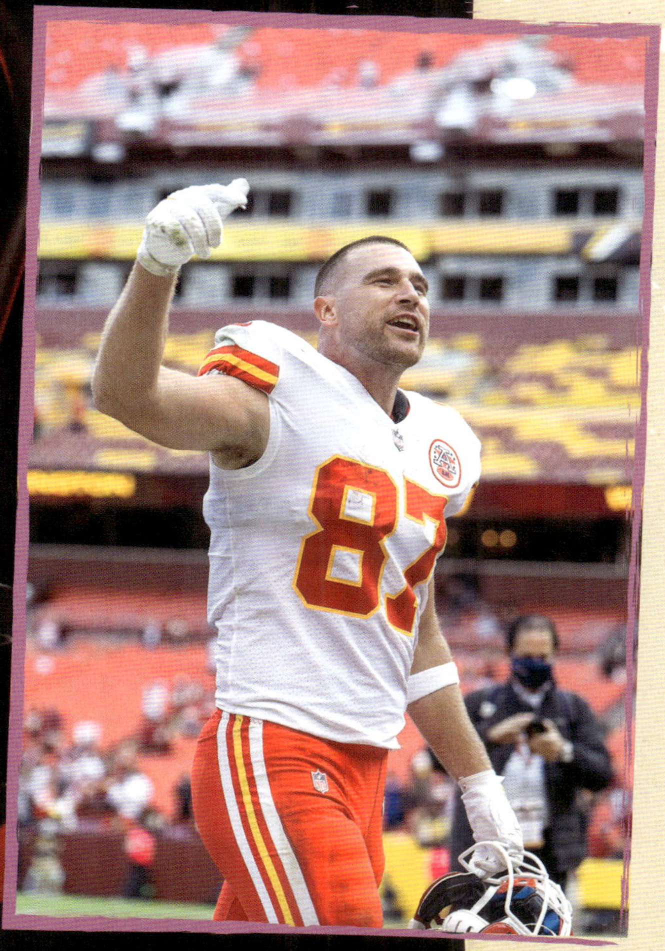

Travis Kelce
July 2023 - present
Karma is the guy on the Chiefs...

In July 2023, Taylor brought her Eras Tour to Arrowhead Stadium in Kansas City—home turf for Travis Kelce, the tight end for the Kansas City Chiefs. Attending the show, the NFL player embarked on a mission of his own, crafting a friendship bracelet with his phone number specifically for Taylor. Since then, the two became an official item and a constant fixture of the media. Taylor has attended several of Travis' games (including the 2024 Super Bowl), and he has visited her on her global Eras Tour stops.

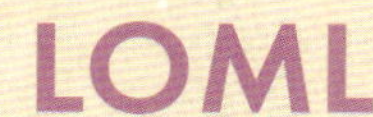

Though Taylor is no stranger to breaking records, she really outdid herself with The Tortured Poets Department. Two hours after its initial release, Taylor dropped a surprise double album called TTPD Anthology, smashing streaming records for Spotify, Apple Music and Amazon combined. Her song Fortnight also became the highest played song in one day ever on Spotify.

Tortured Poets is an album for her fans, as we see Taylor bare her soul, just as she had done when she first started her wild journey 17 years ago...

Spotify's Taylor Swift pop-up at The Grove for her new album "The Tortured Poets Department" at The Grove on April 16, 2024 in Los Angeles, California

STELLAR SINGLE
Fortnight

The album's first track features Post Malone sharing an enjoyable back-and-forth with Taylor. This song is rumoured to be about her relationship with Matty Healy, as she tried to move on from her long-term boyfriend Joe Alwyn by getting involved with someone else. If the song wasn't so dark and dreary, it could easily fit on the album "Midnights."

Taylor Swift during the 2022 American Music Awards at Microsoft Theater on November 20, 2022 in Los Angeles

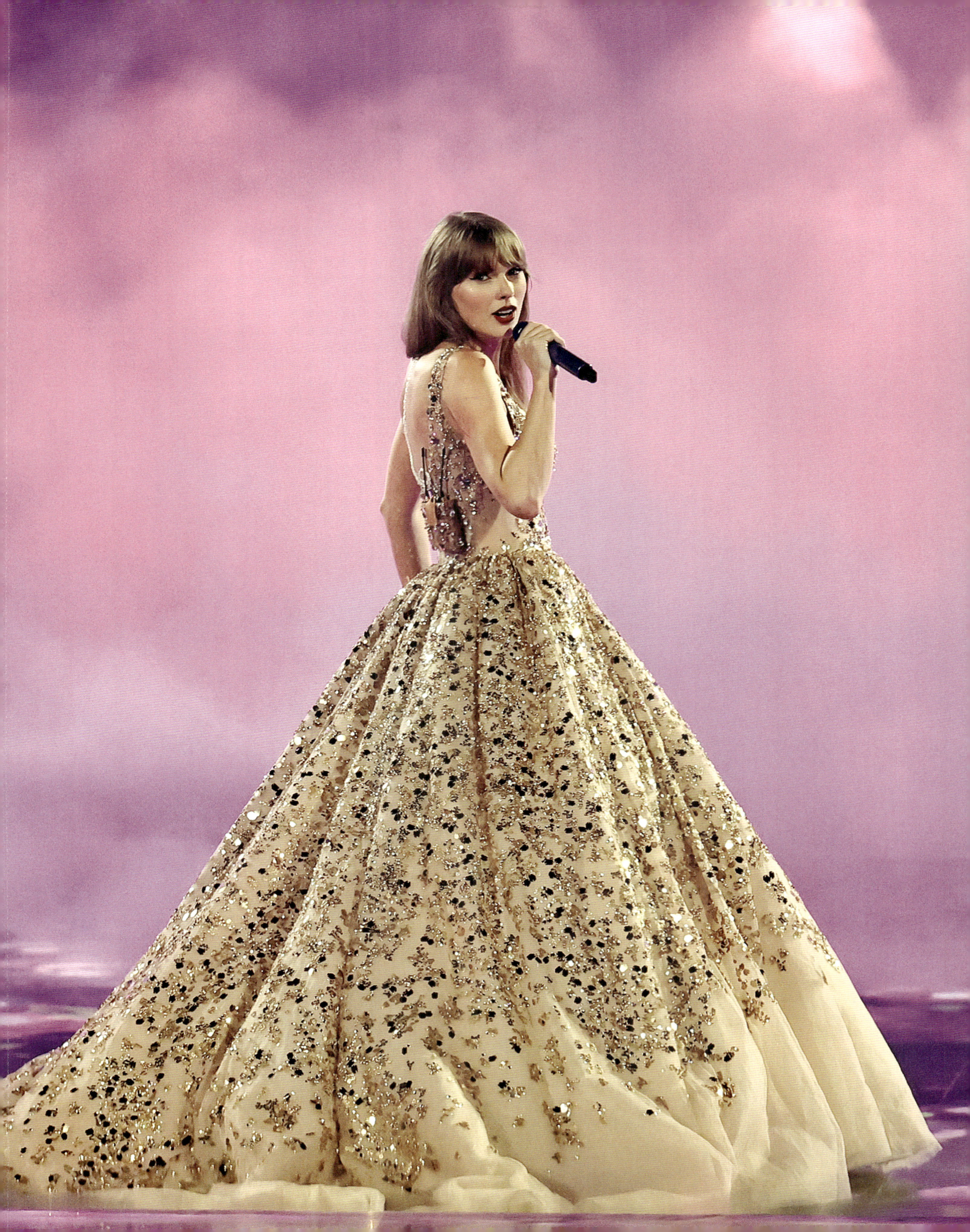

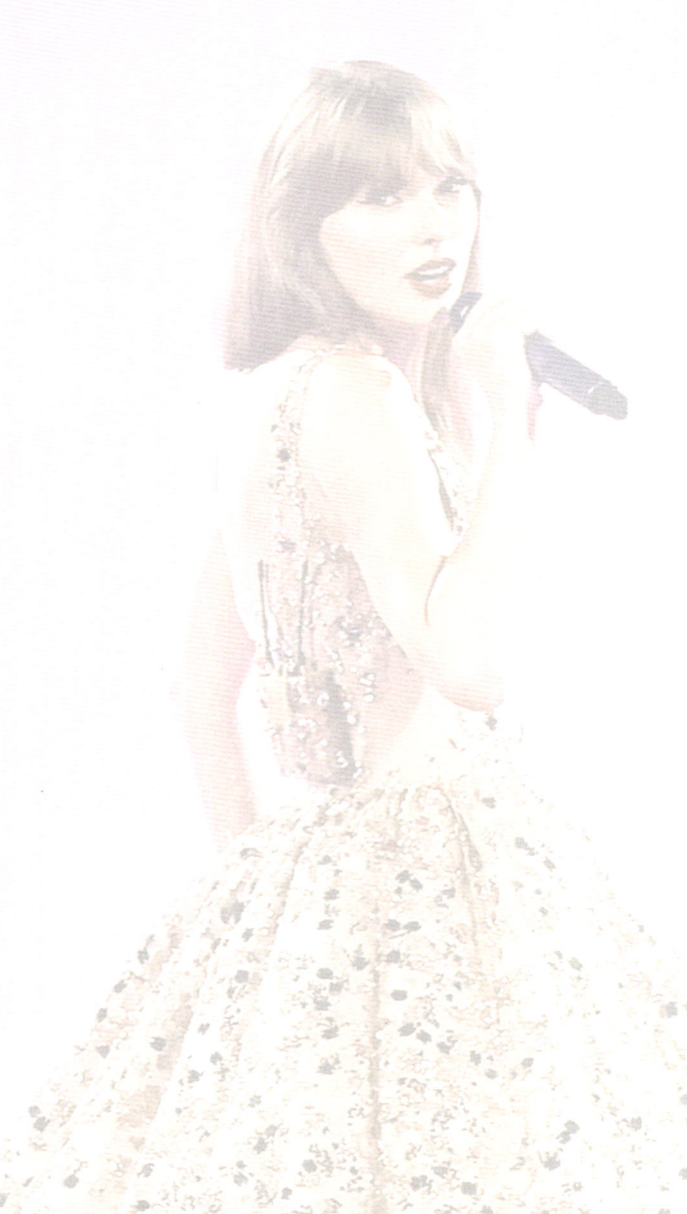

Taylor Swift performs onstage during
The Eras Tour at NRG Stadium on
April 21, 2023 in Houston, Texas

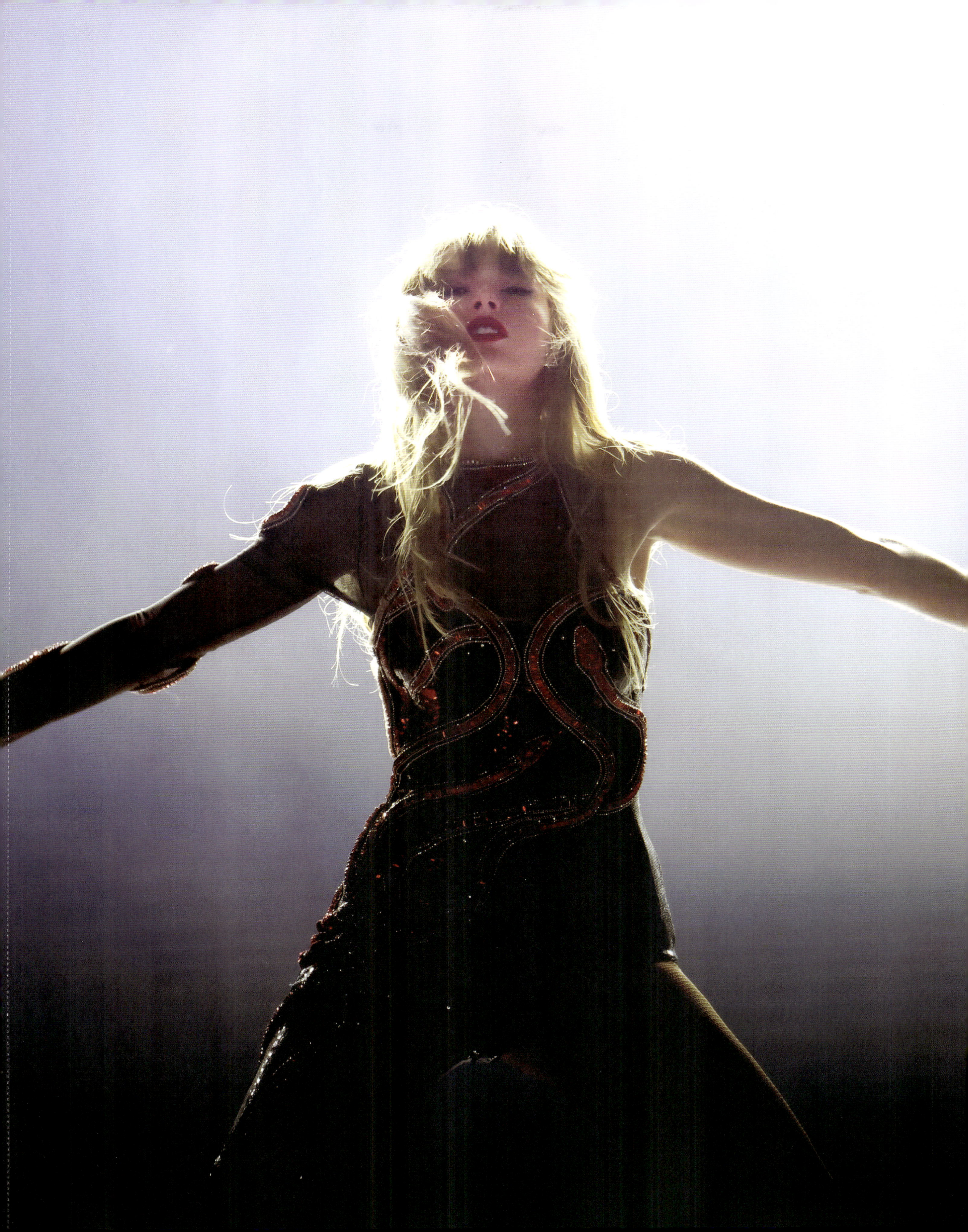

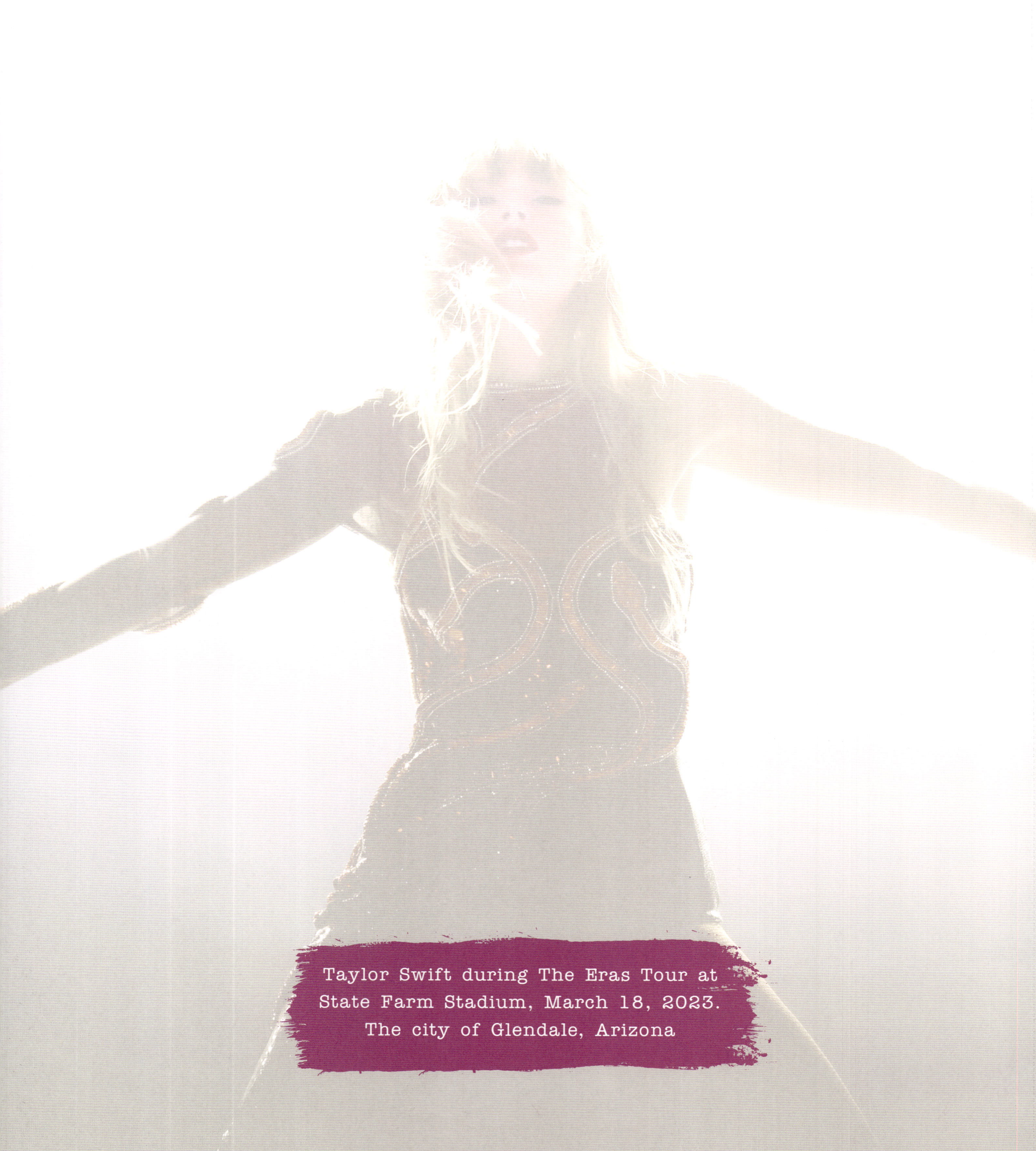

Taylor Swift during The Eras Tour at State Farm Stadium, March 18, 2023. The city of Glendale, Arizona

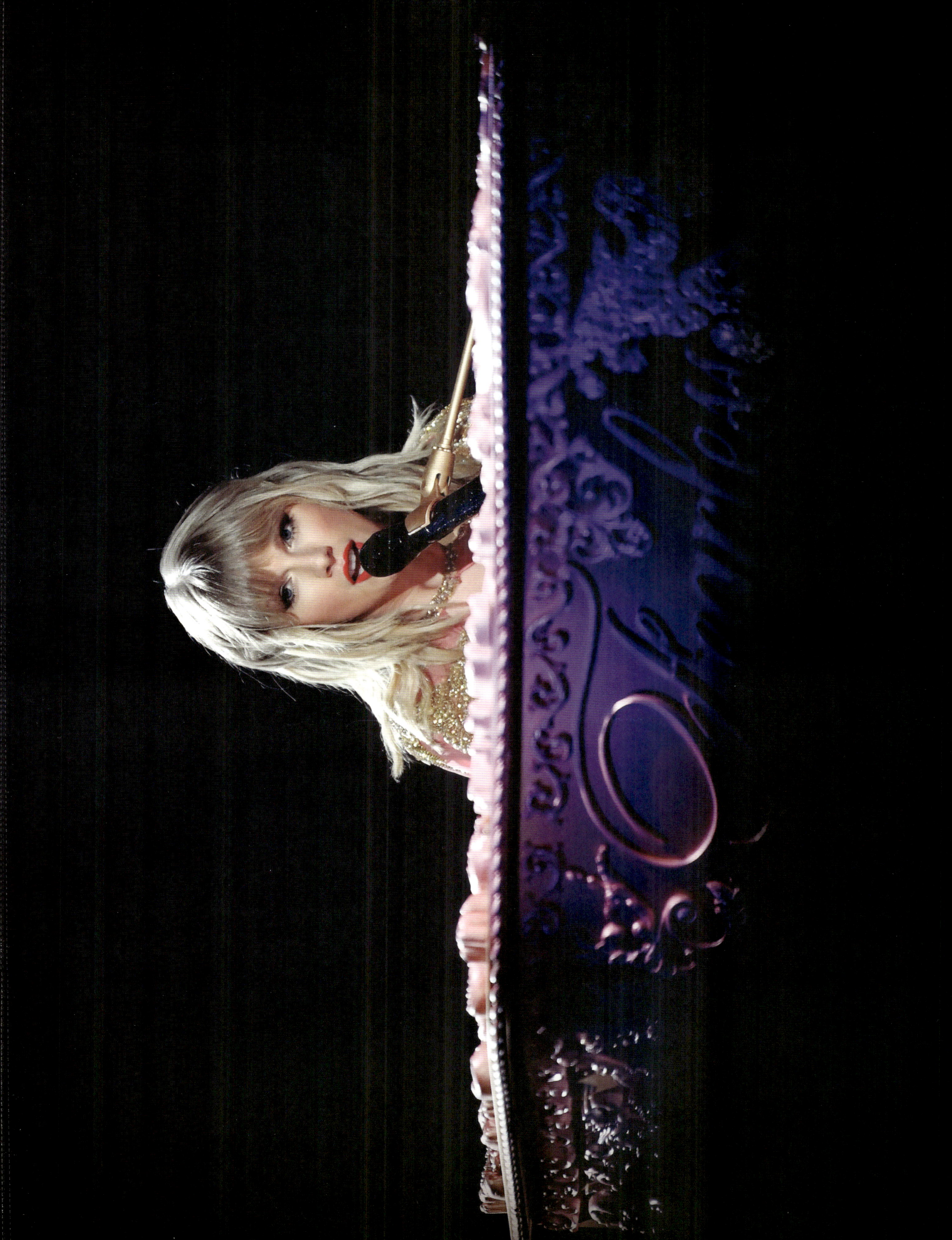

Taylor Swift onstage during the 2019 American Music Awards, November 24, 2019 in Los Angeles, California

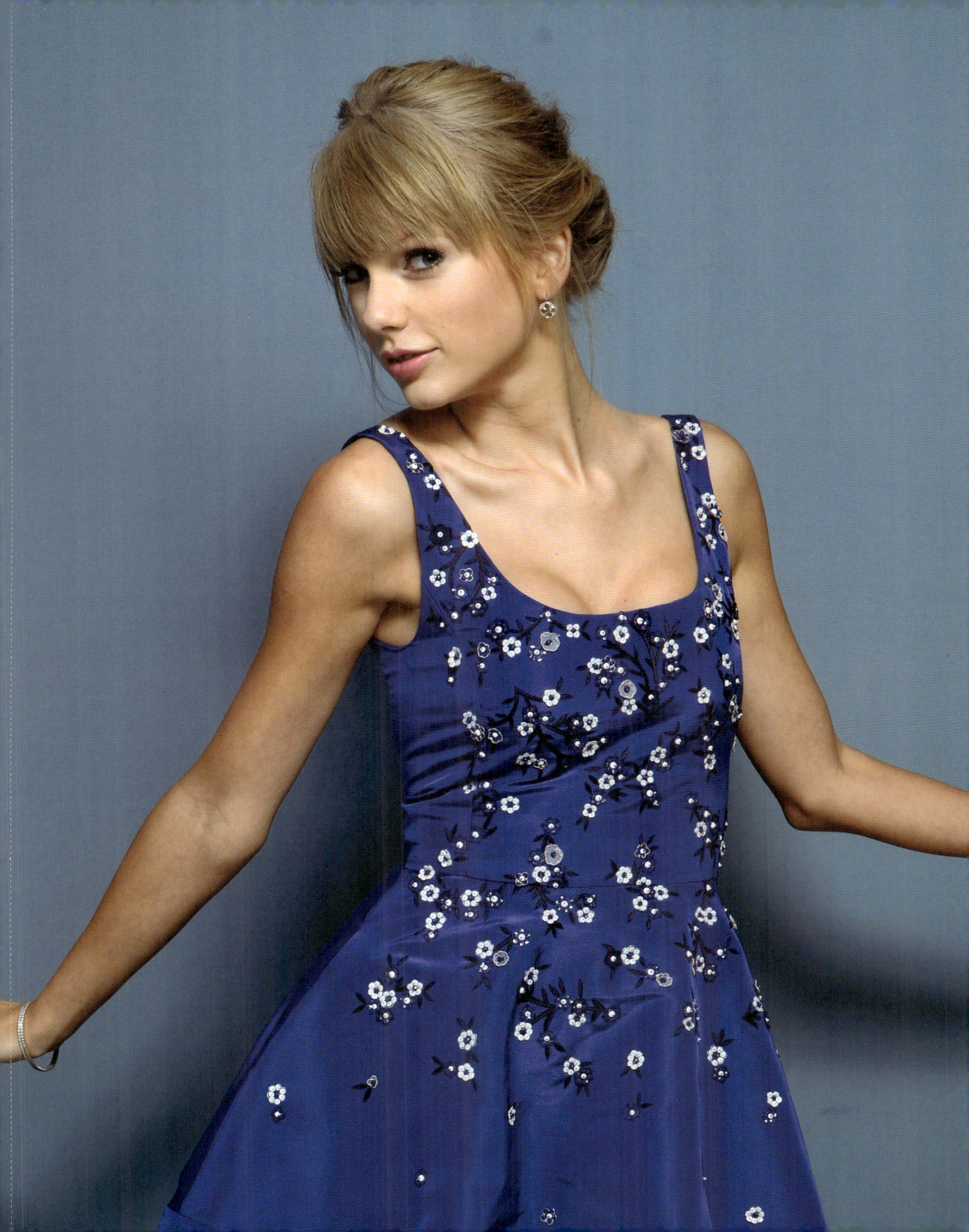

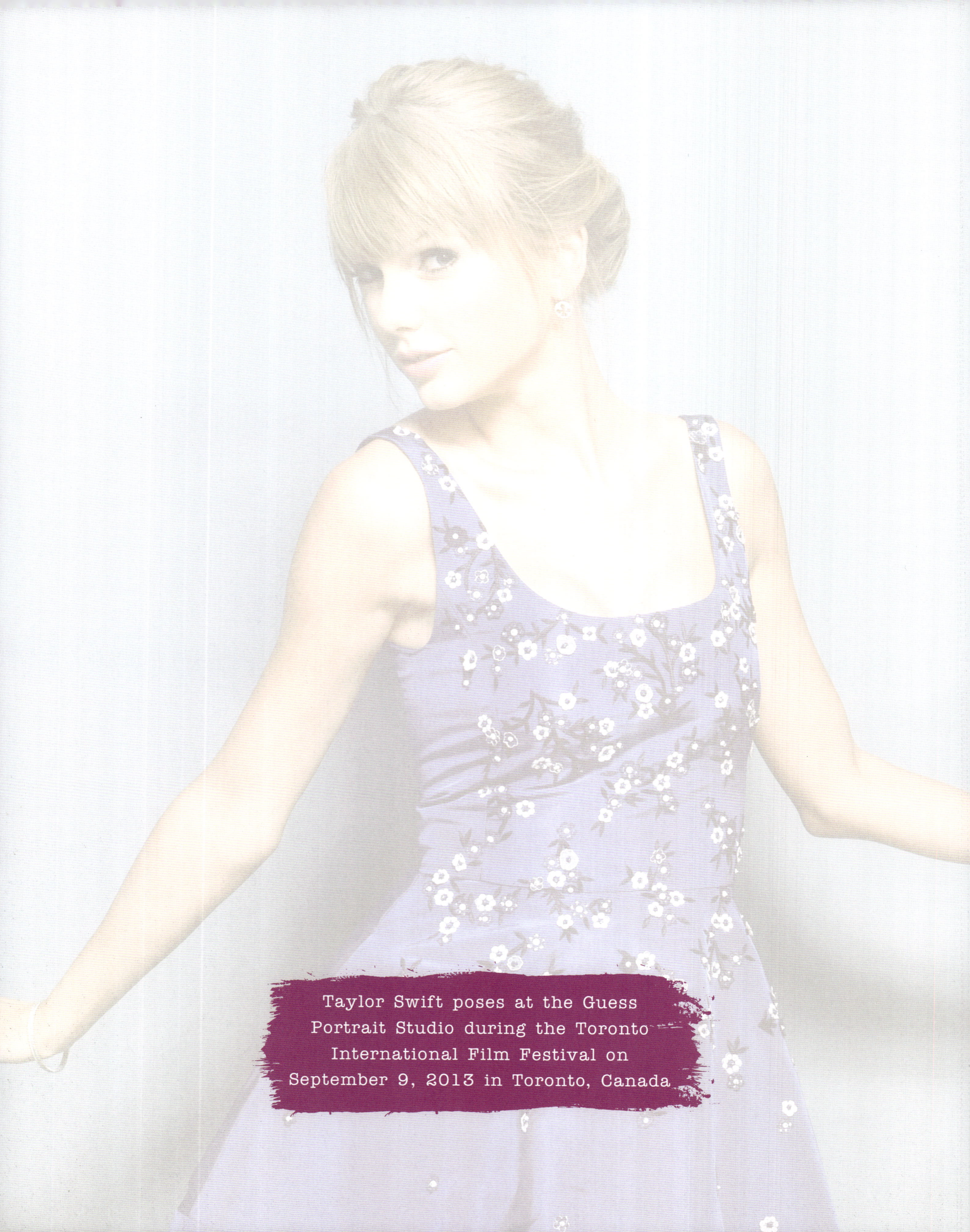

Taylor Swift poses at the Guess Portrait Studio during the Toronto International Film Festival on September 9, 2013 in Toronto, Canada

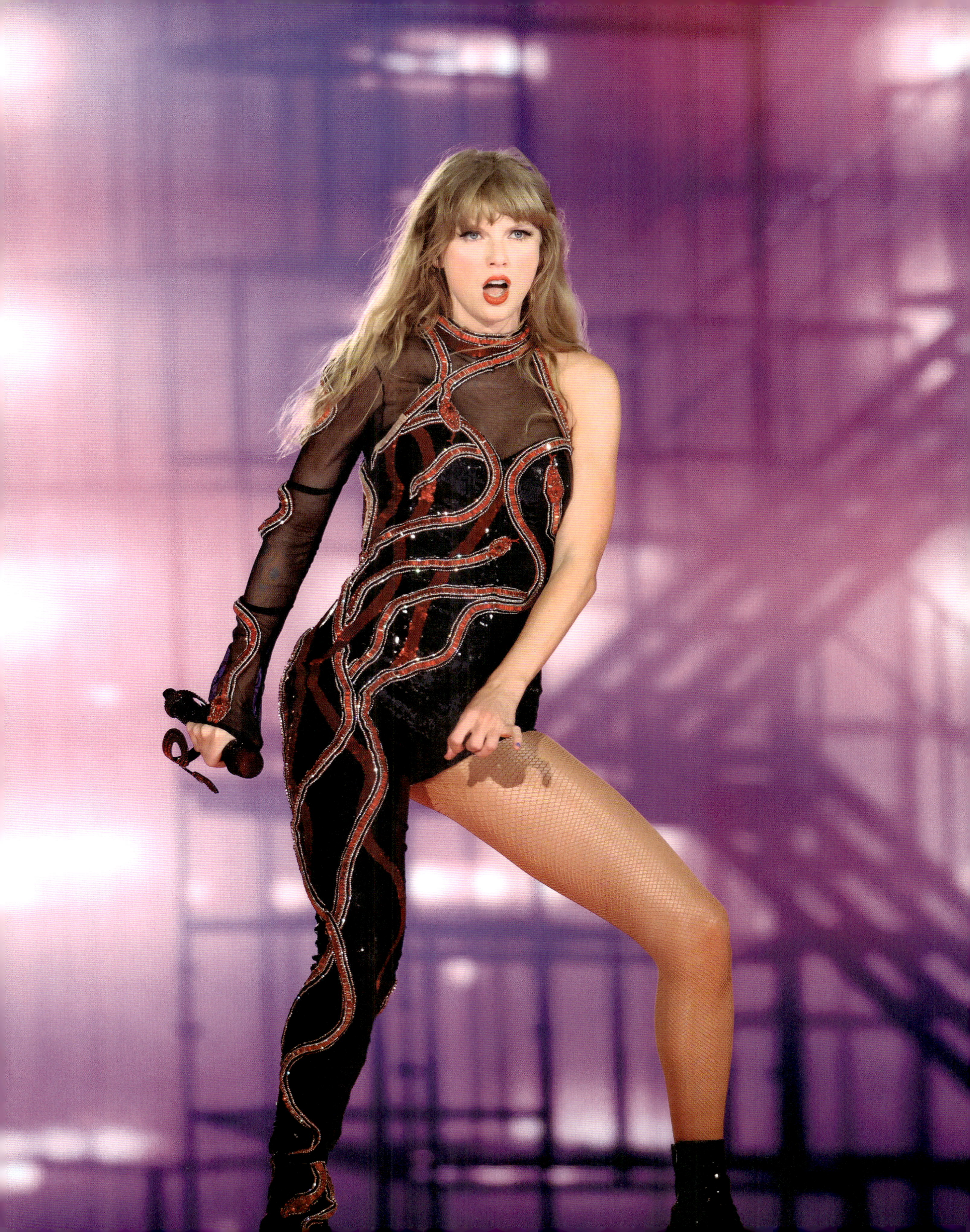

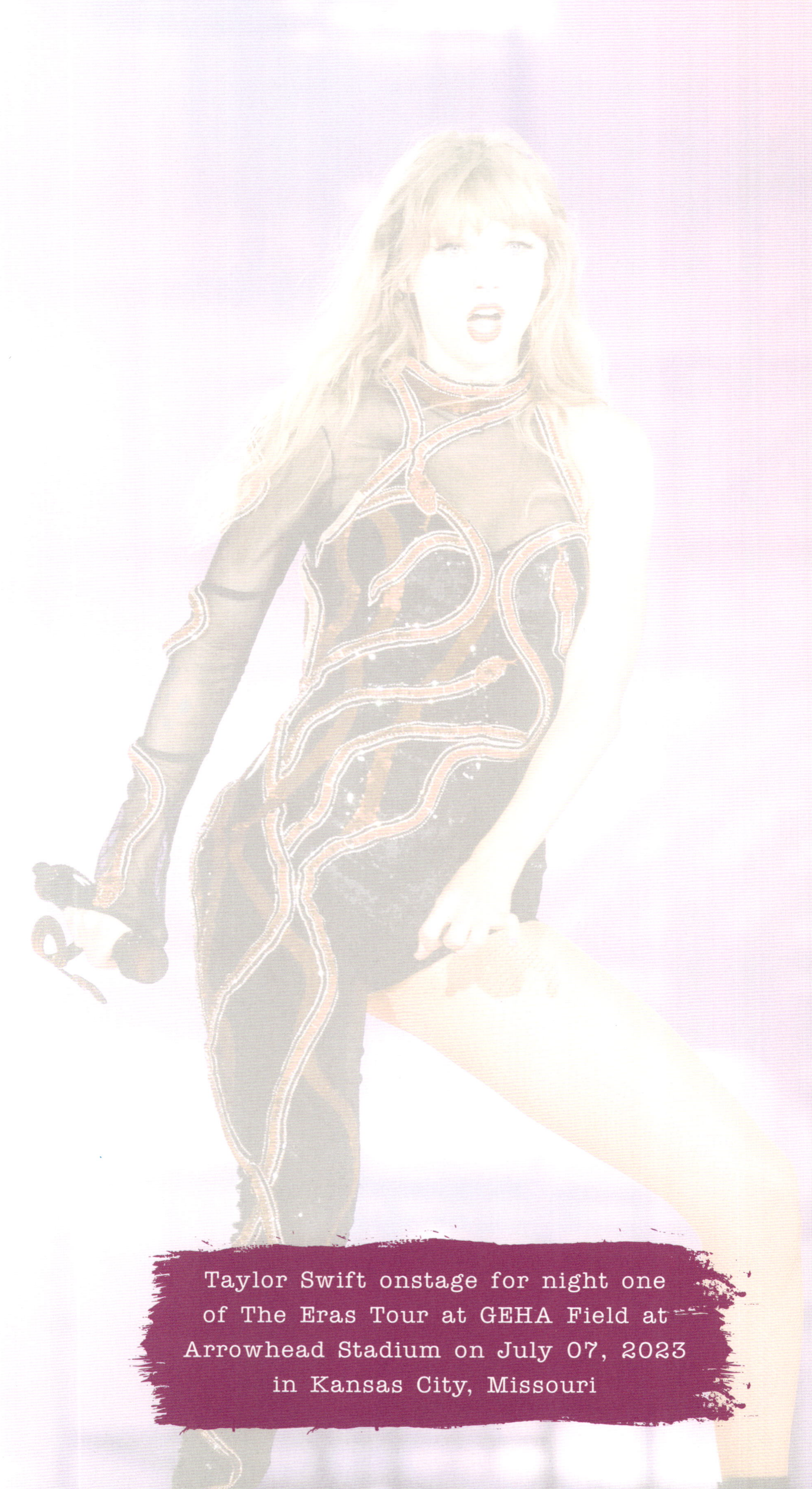

Taylor Swift onstage for night one of The Eras Tour at GEHA Field at Arrowhead Stadium on July 07, 2023 in Kansas City, Missouri

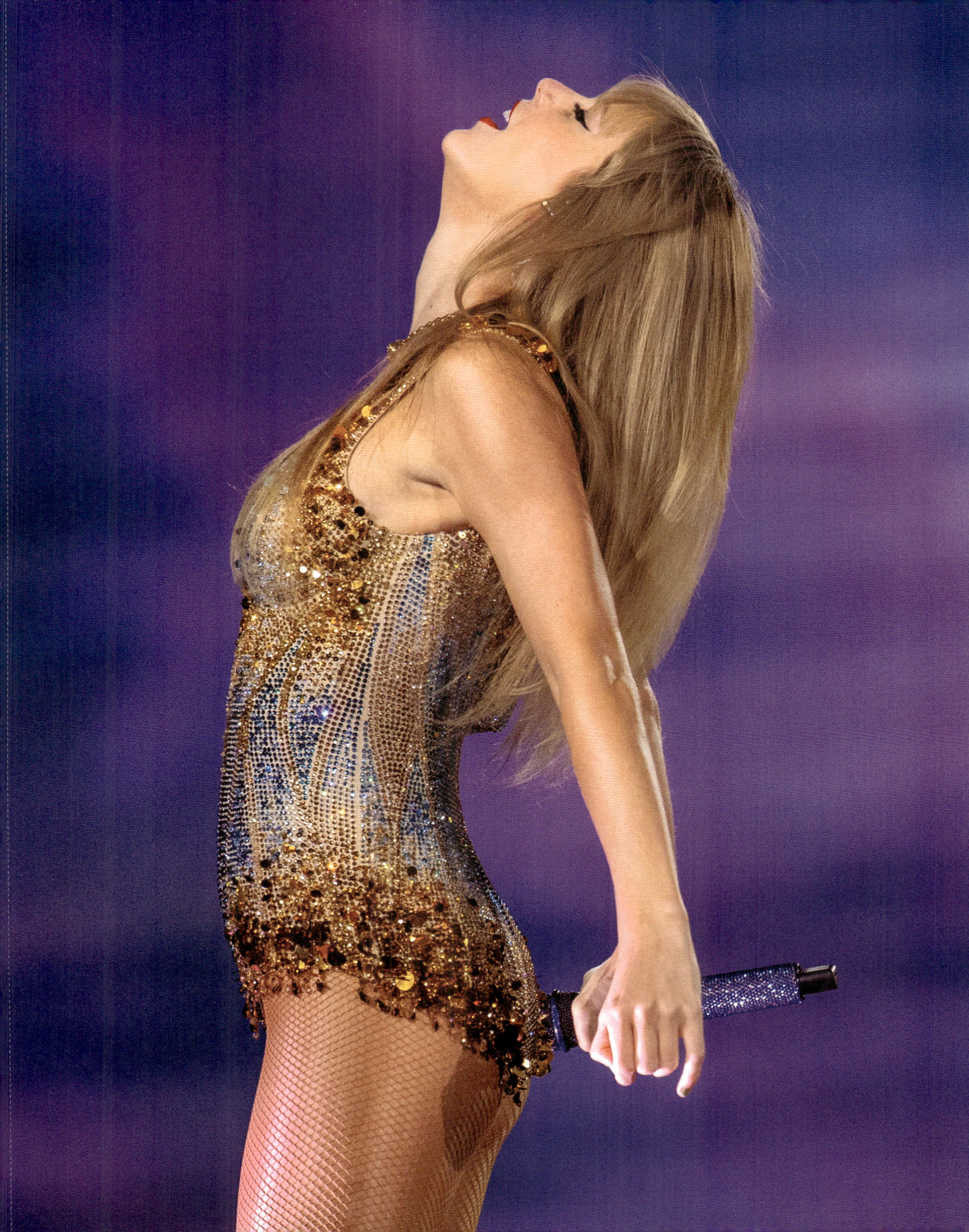

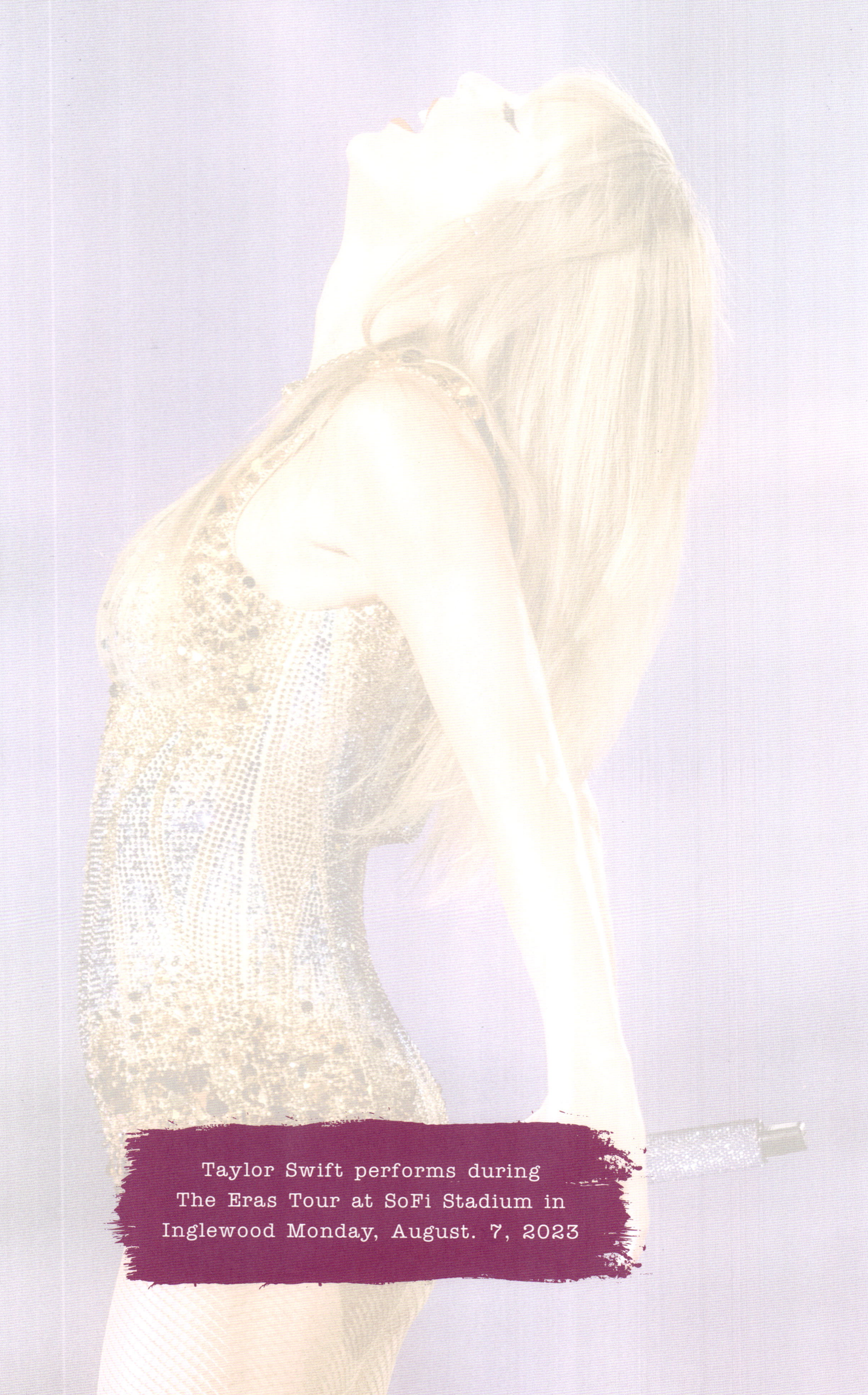

Taylor Swift performs during
The Eras Tour at SoFi Stadium in
Inglewood Monday, August. 7, 2023

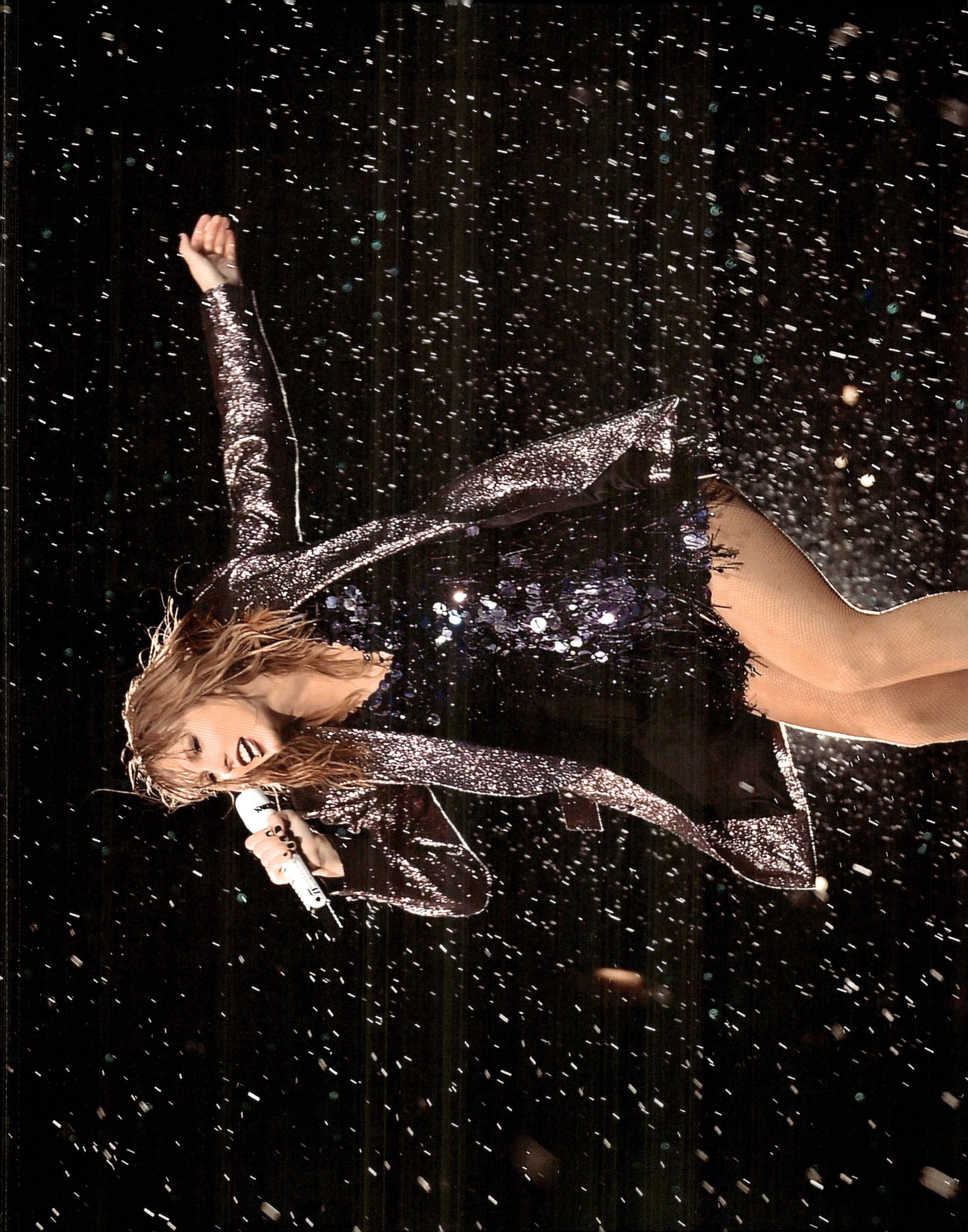

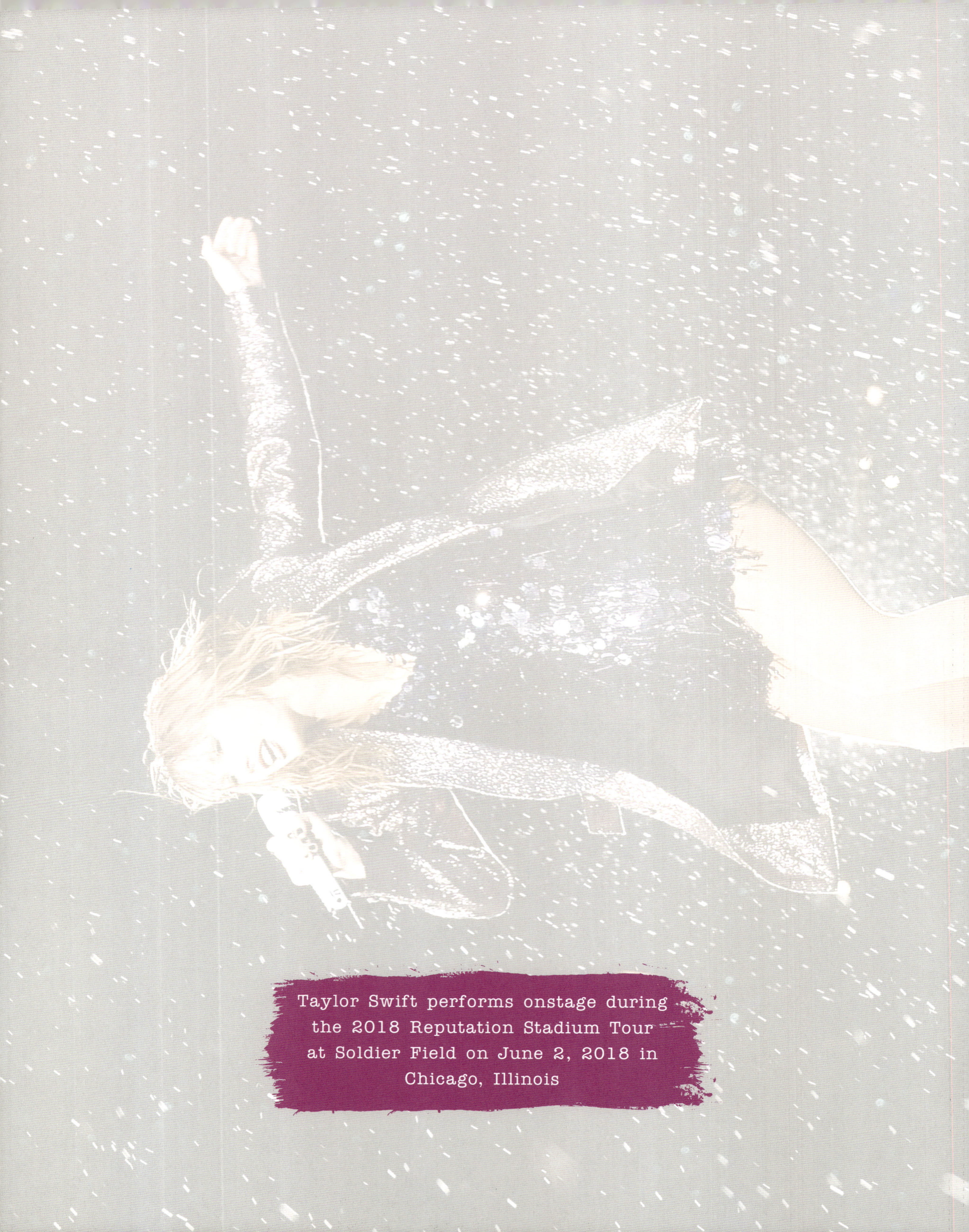

Taylor Swift performs onstage during
the 2018 Reputation Stadium Tour
at Soldier Field on June 2, 2018 in
Chicago, Illinois

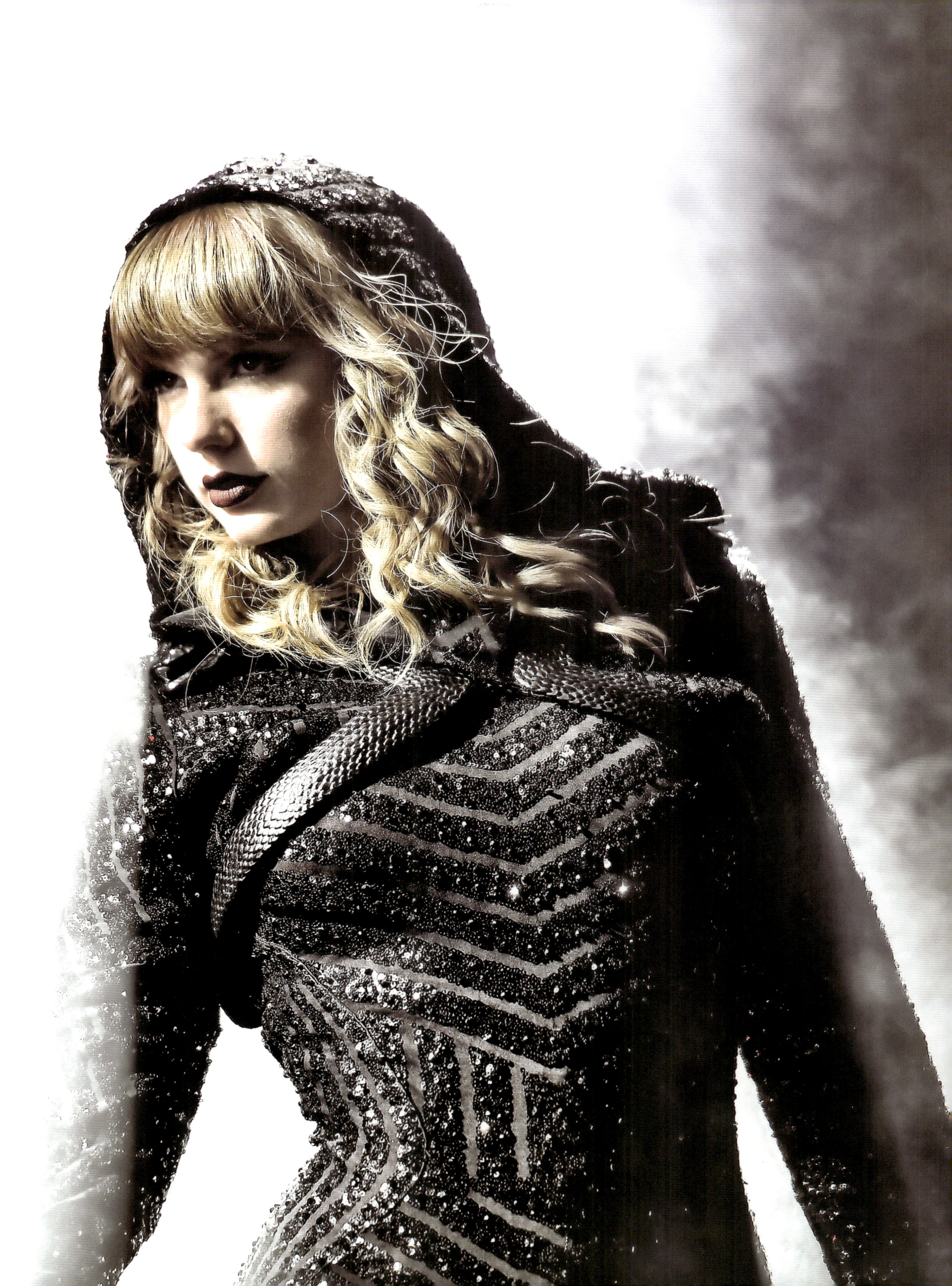

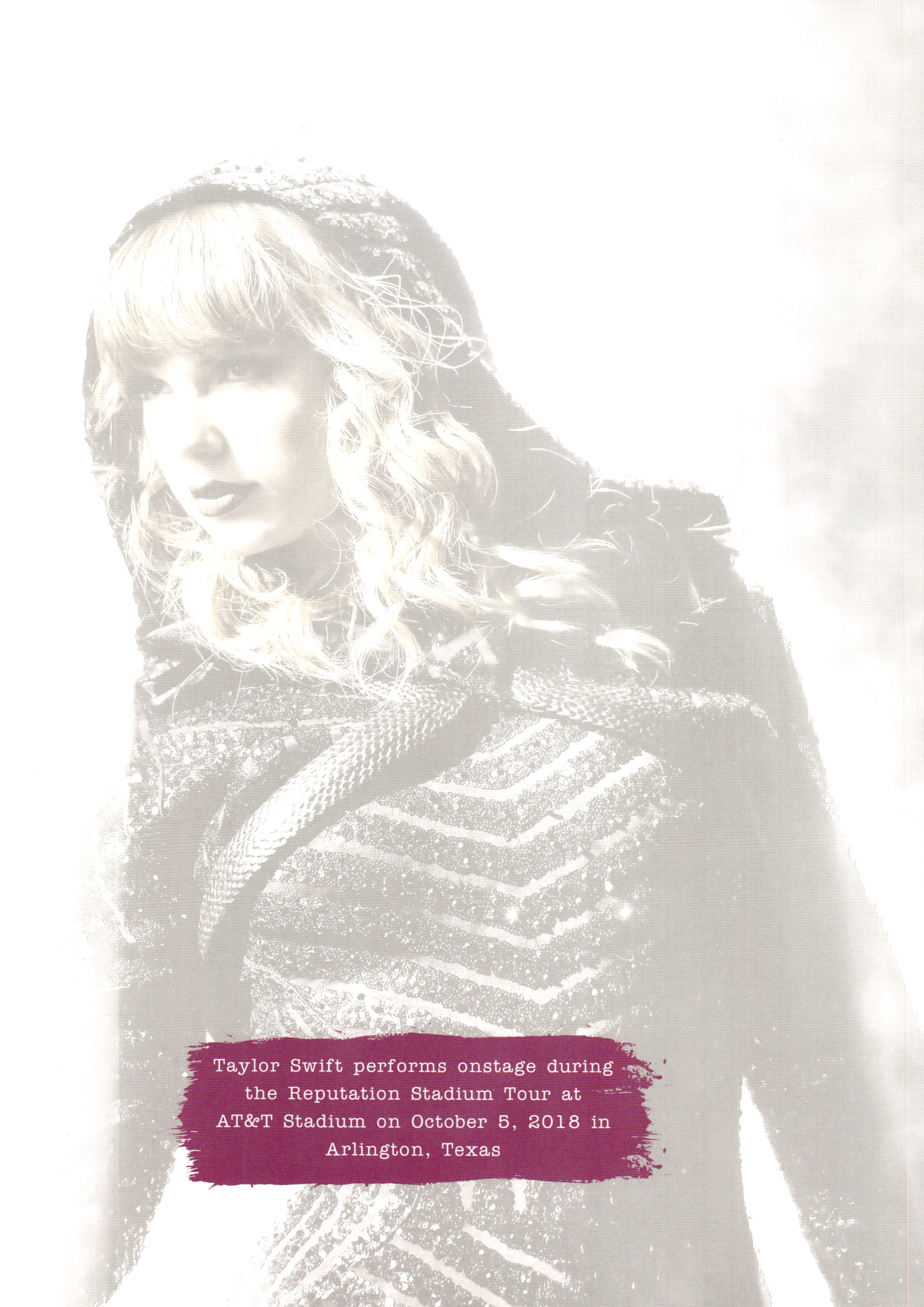

Taylor Swift performs onstage during
the Reputation Stadium Tour at
AT&T Stadium on October 5, 2018 in
Arlington, Texas

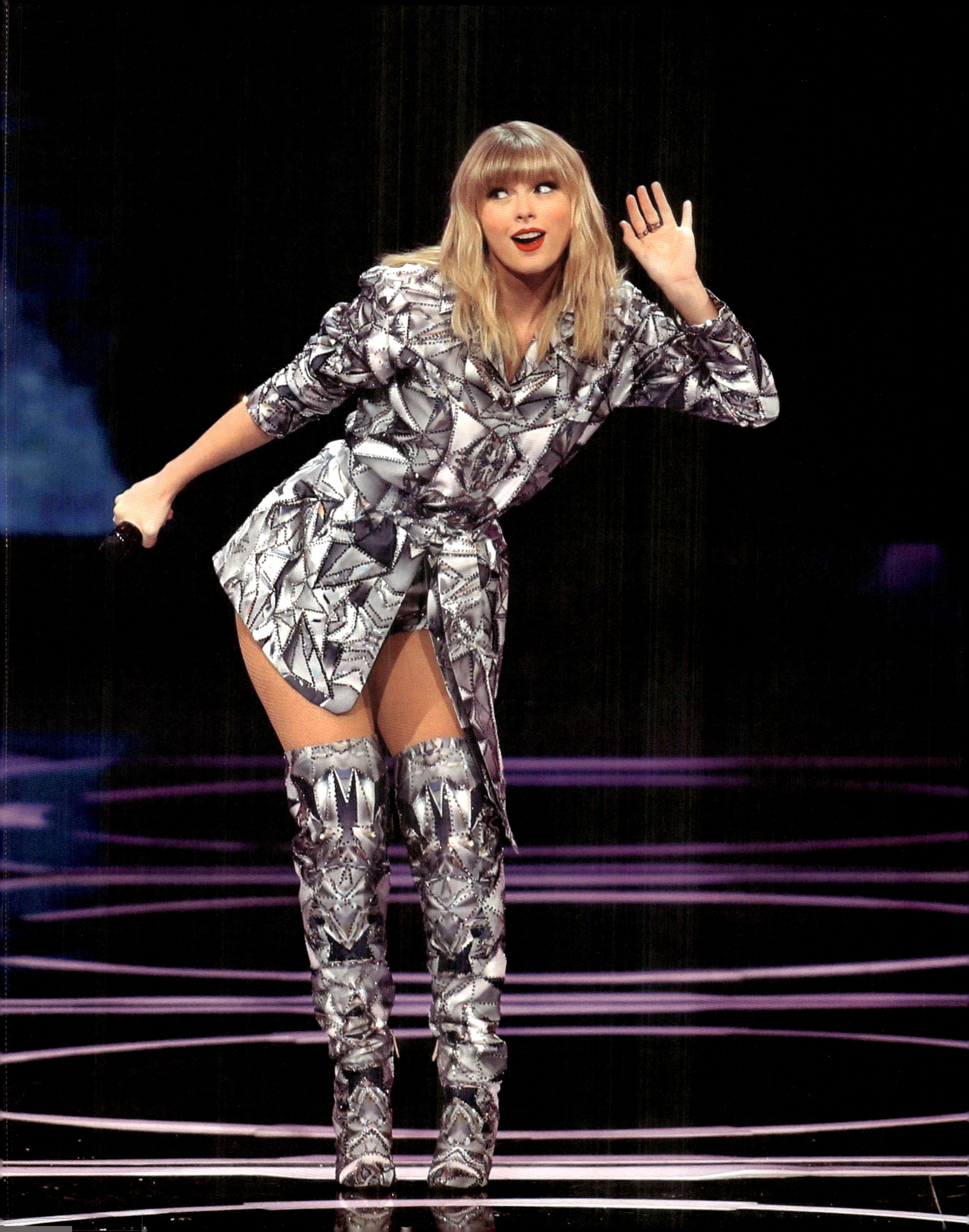

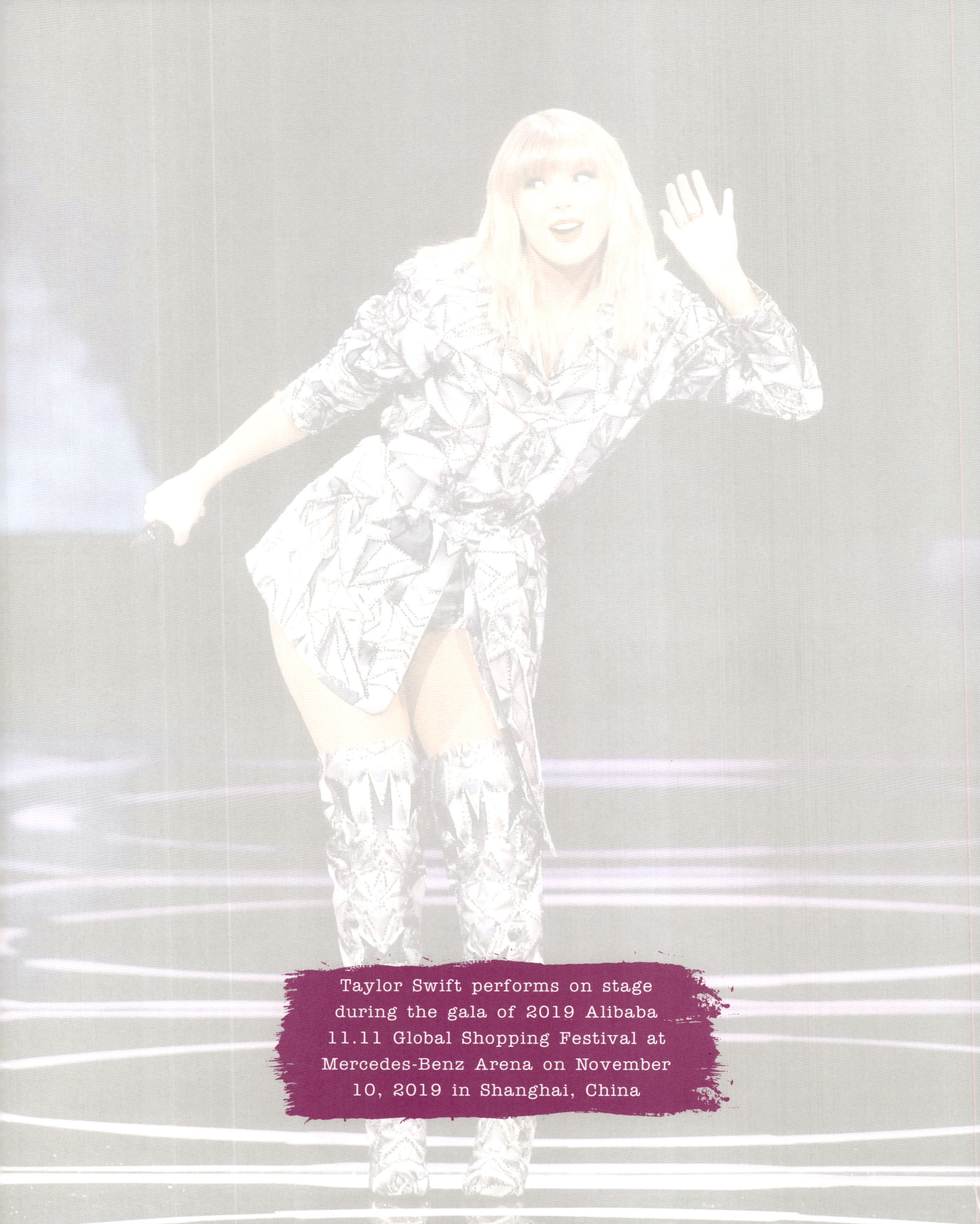

Taylor Swift performs on stage during the gala of 2019 Alibaba 11.11 Global Shopping Festival at Mercedes-Benz Arena on November 10, 2019 in Shanghai, China

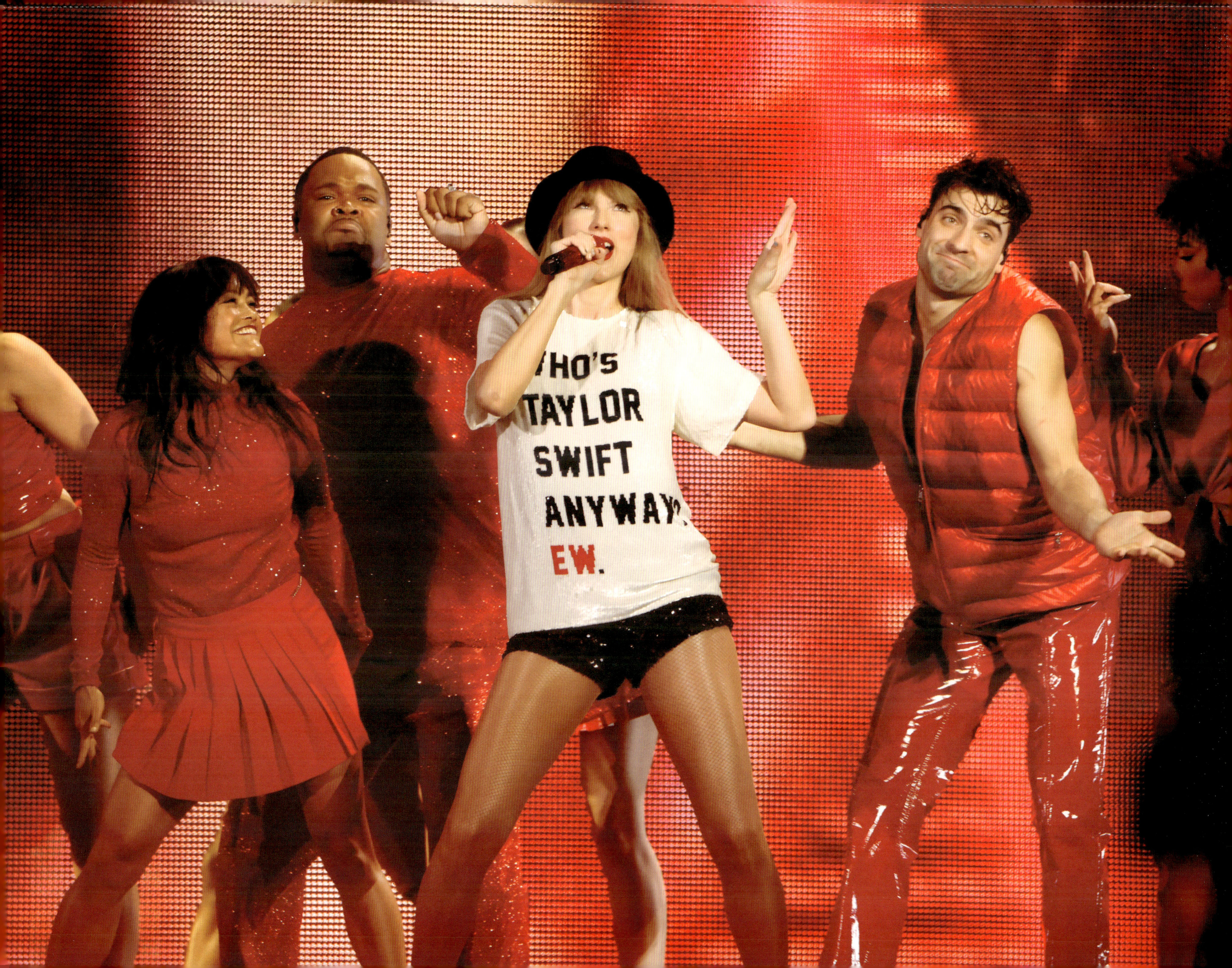
WHO'S
TAYLOR
SWIFT
ANYWAY?
EW.

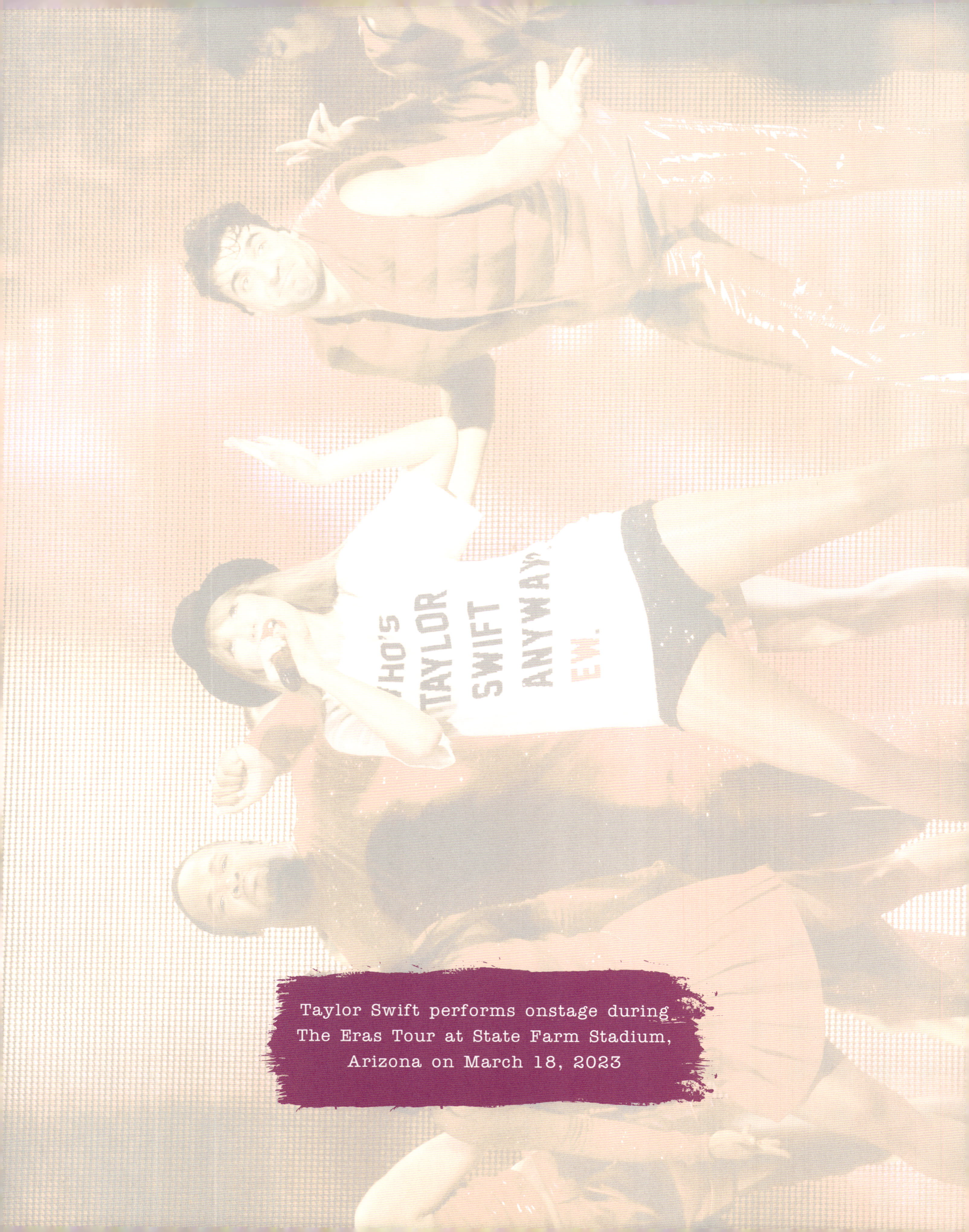

Taylor Swift performs onstage during The Eras Tour at State Farm Stadium, Arizona on March 18, 2023

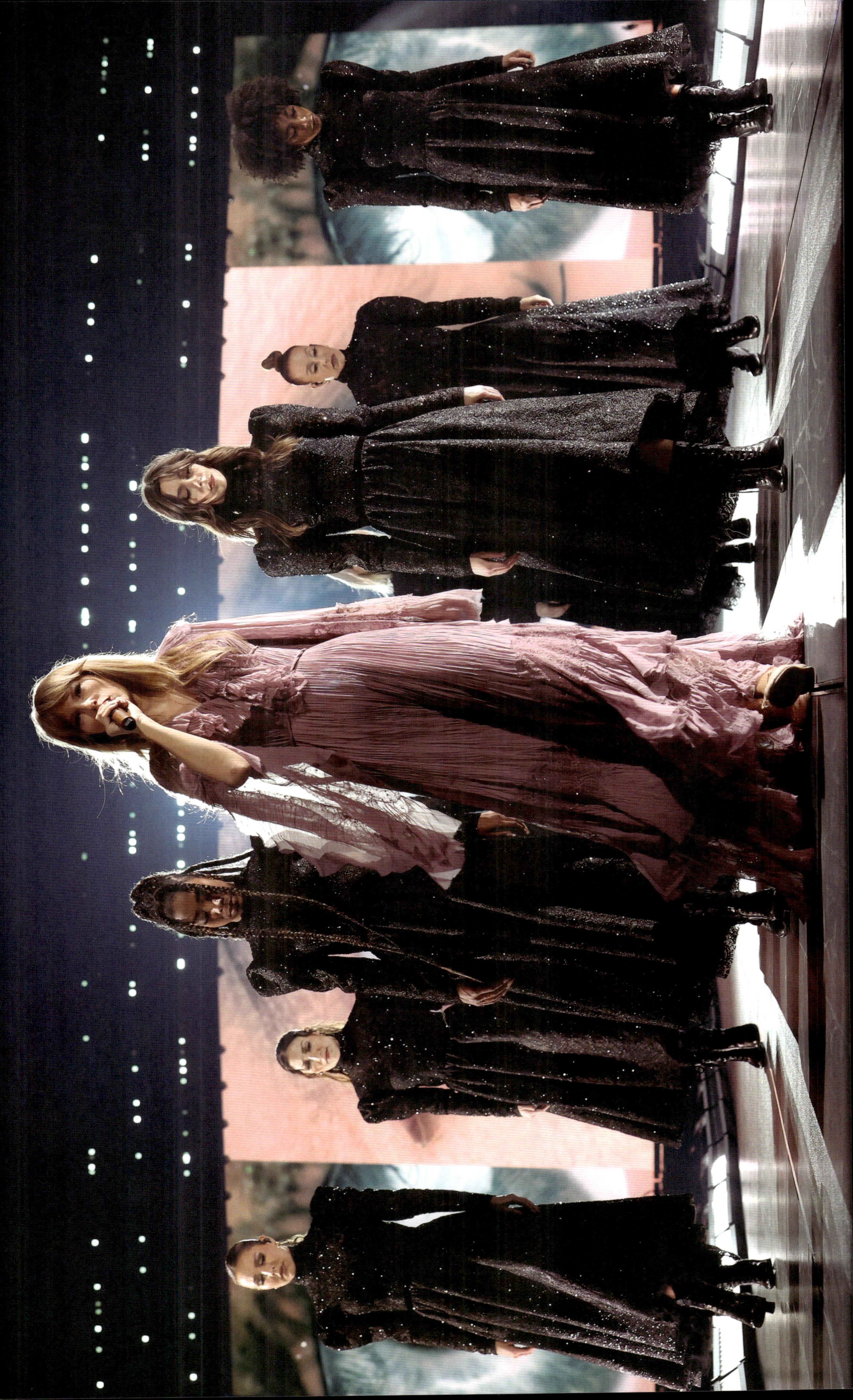

Taylor Swift performs onstage during The Eras Tour at State Farm Stadium, Arizona on March 18, 2023

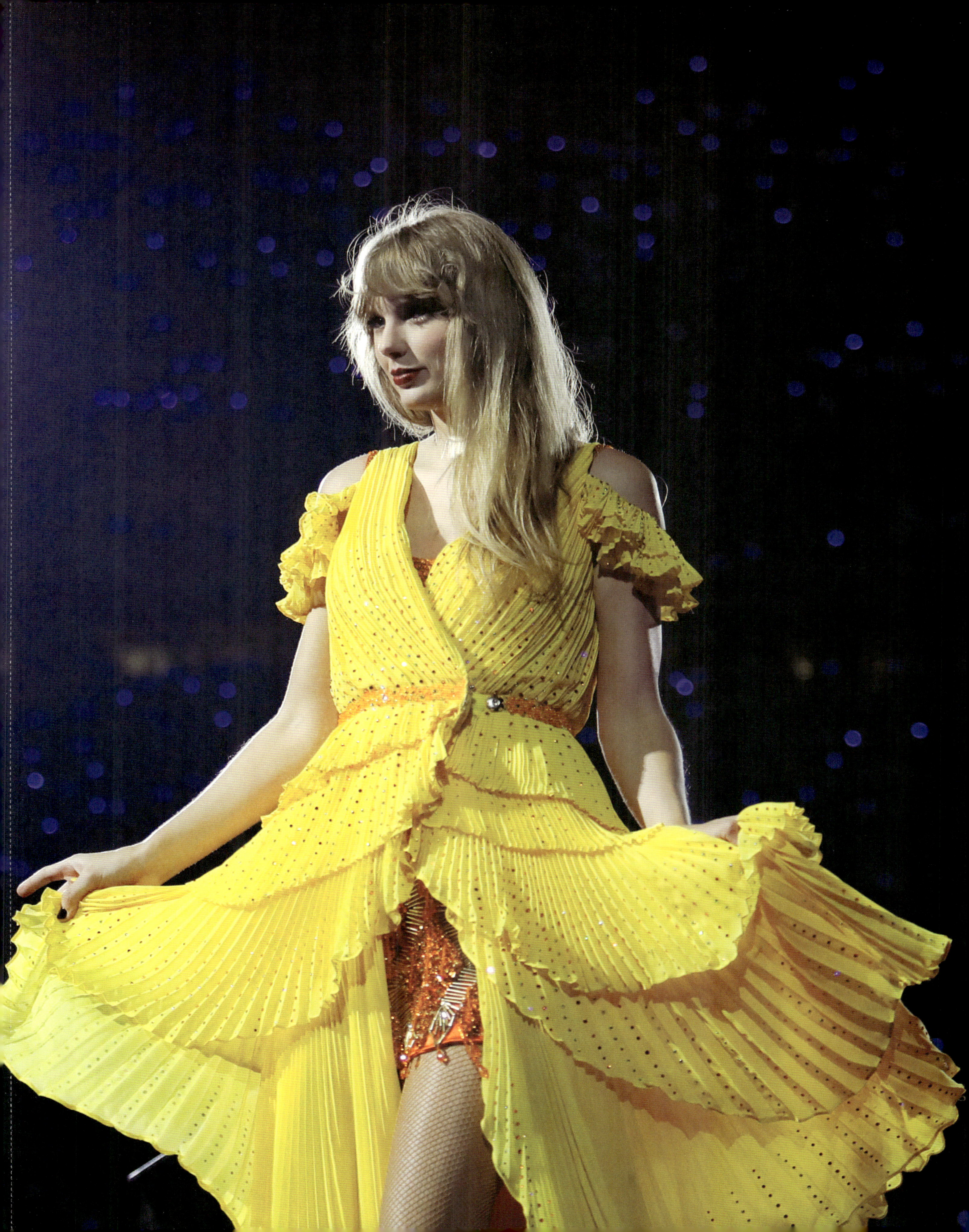

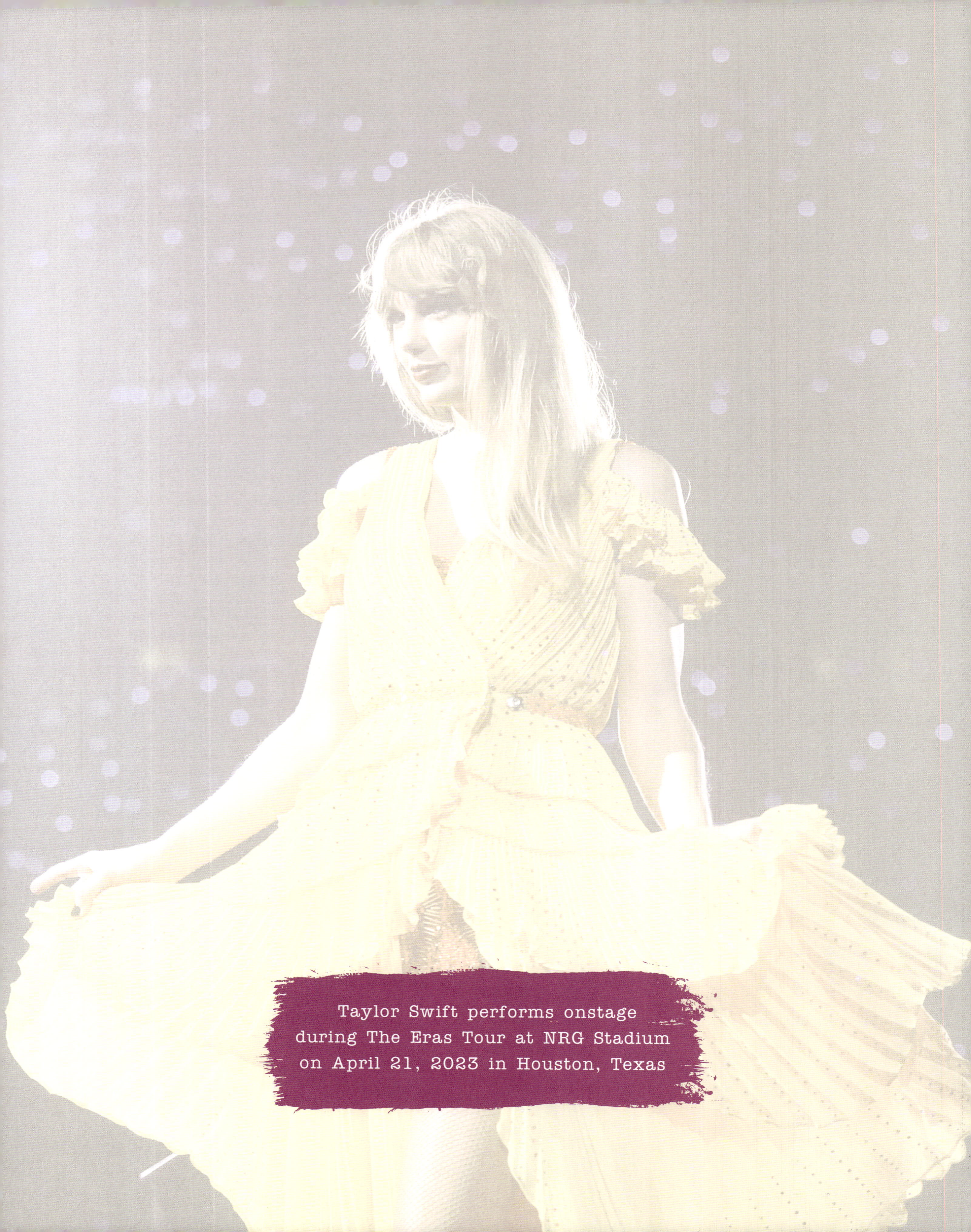

Taylor Swift performs onstage
during The Eras Tour at NRG Stadium
on April 21, 2023 in Houston, Texas

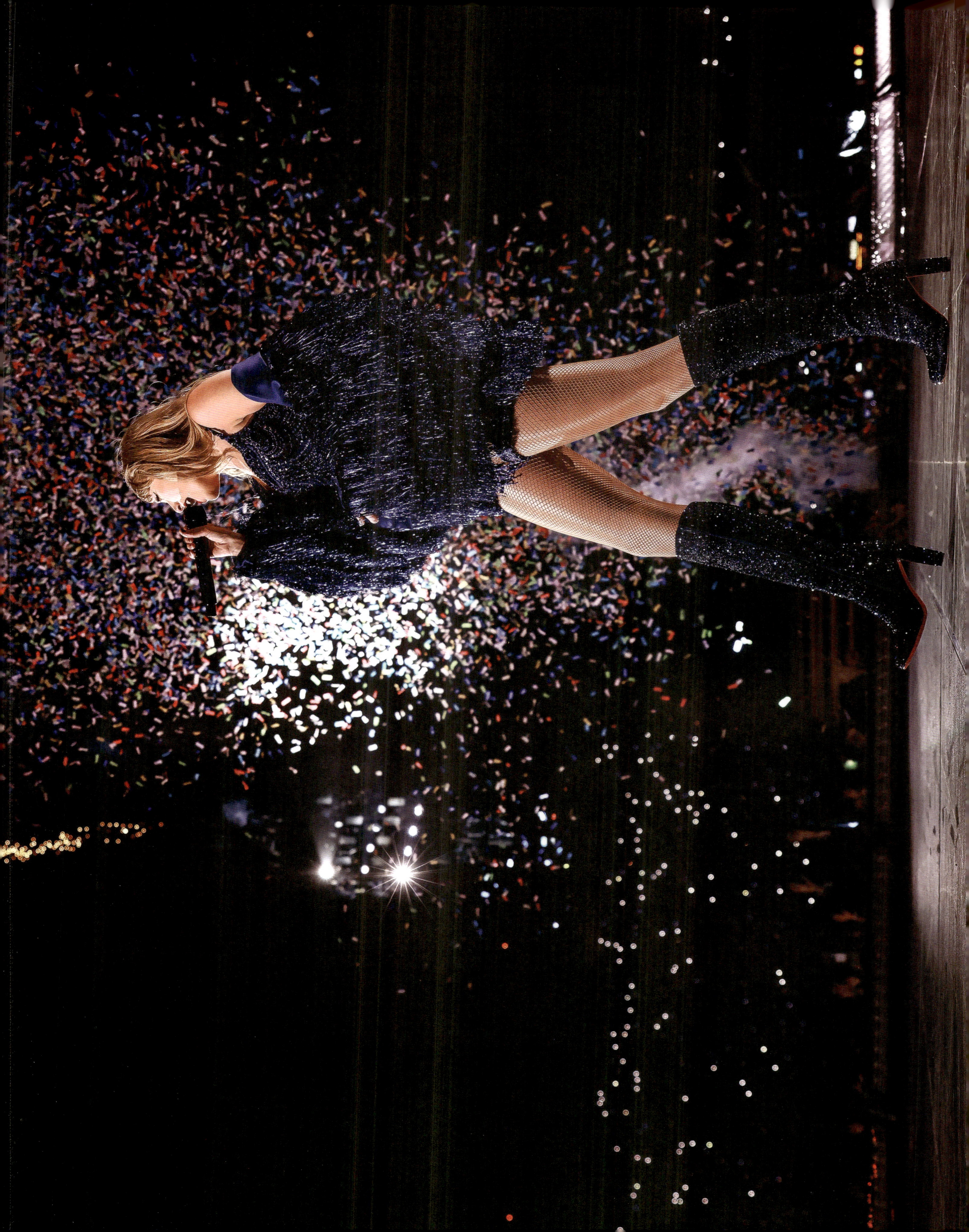

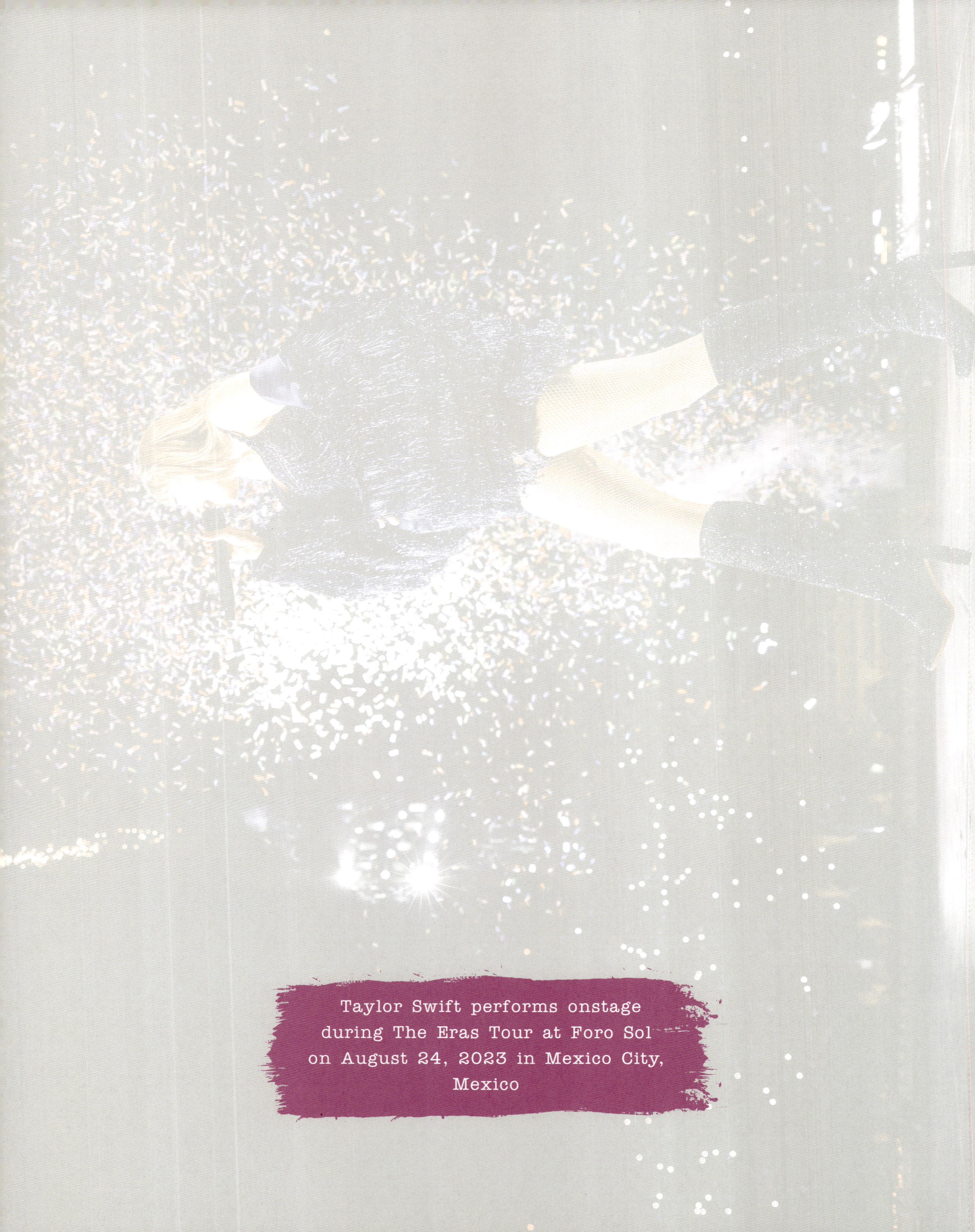

Taylor Swift performs onstage during The Eras Tour at Foro Sol on August 24, 2023 in Mexico City, Mexico

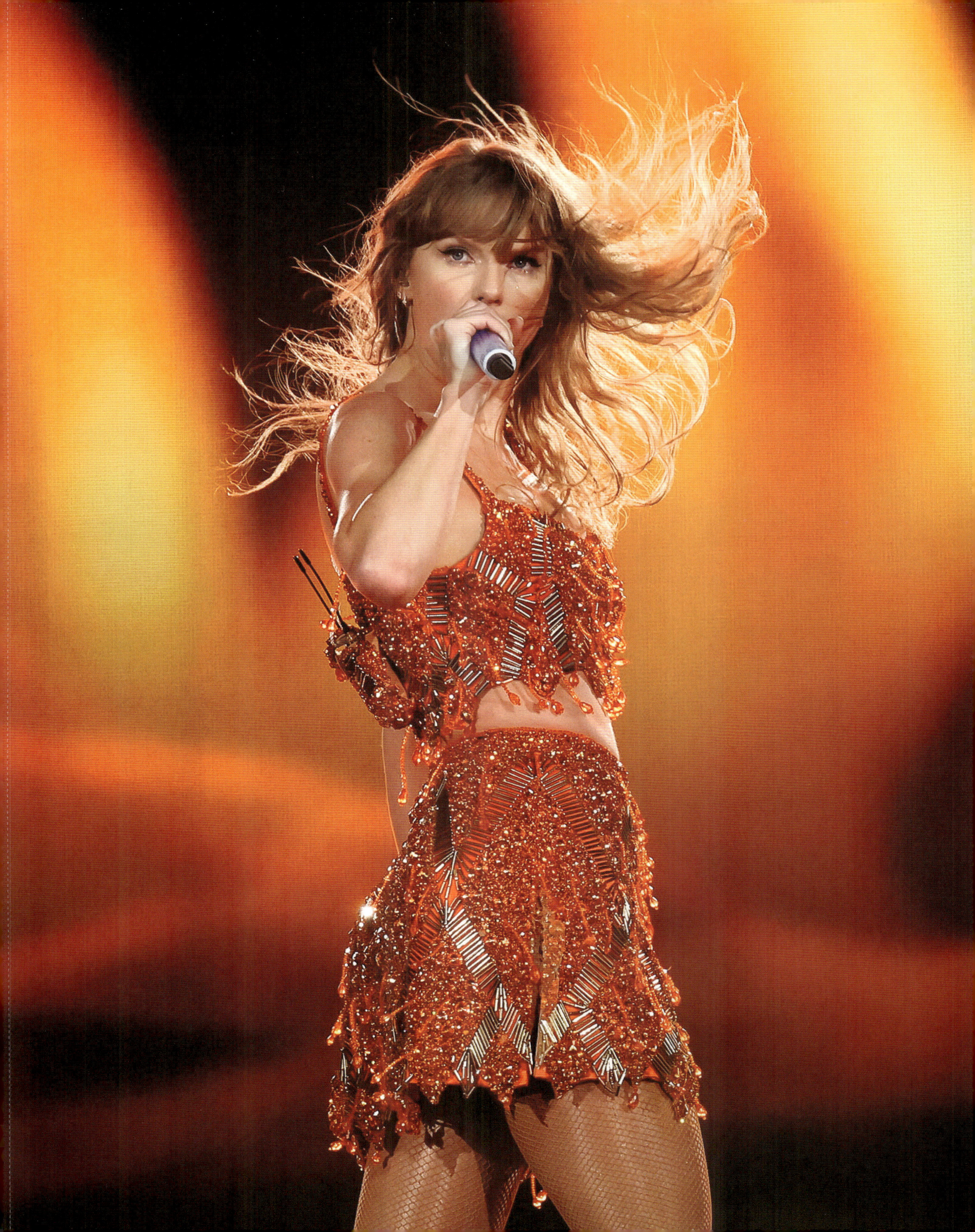

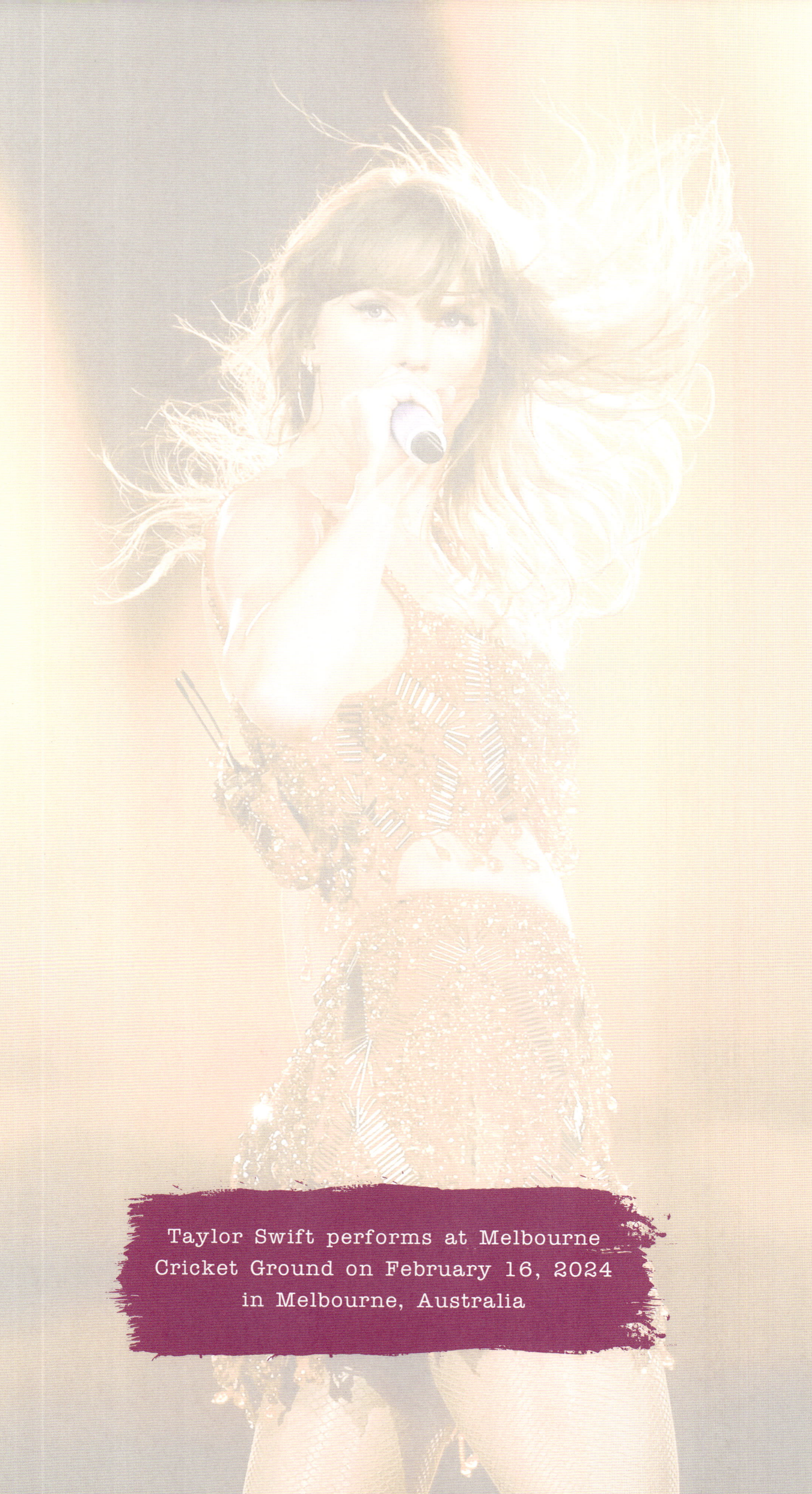

Taylor Swift performs at Melbourne Cricket Ground on February 16, 2024 in Melbourne, Australia

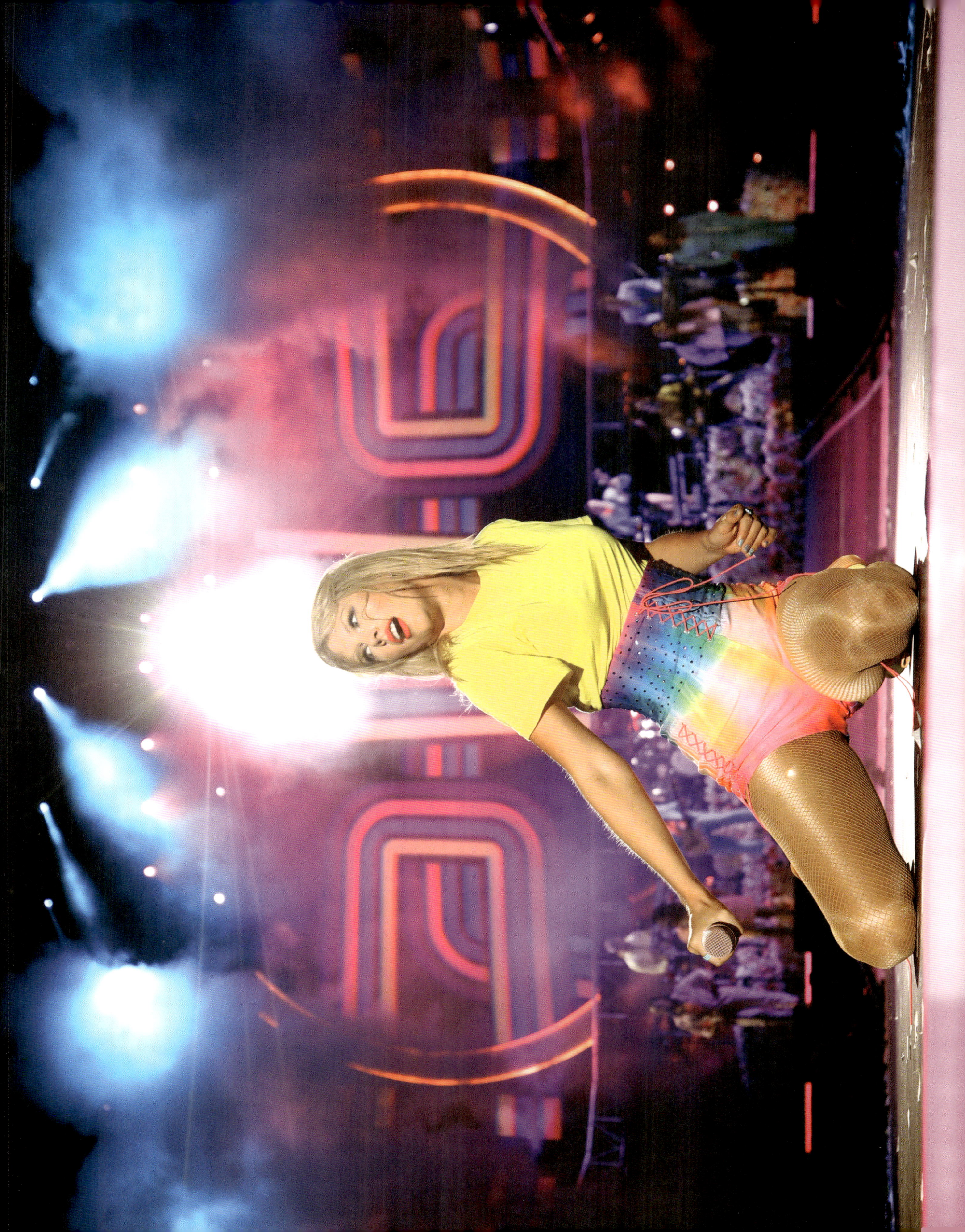

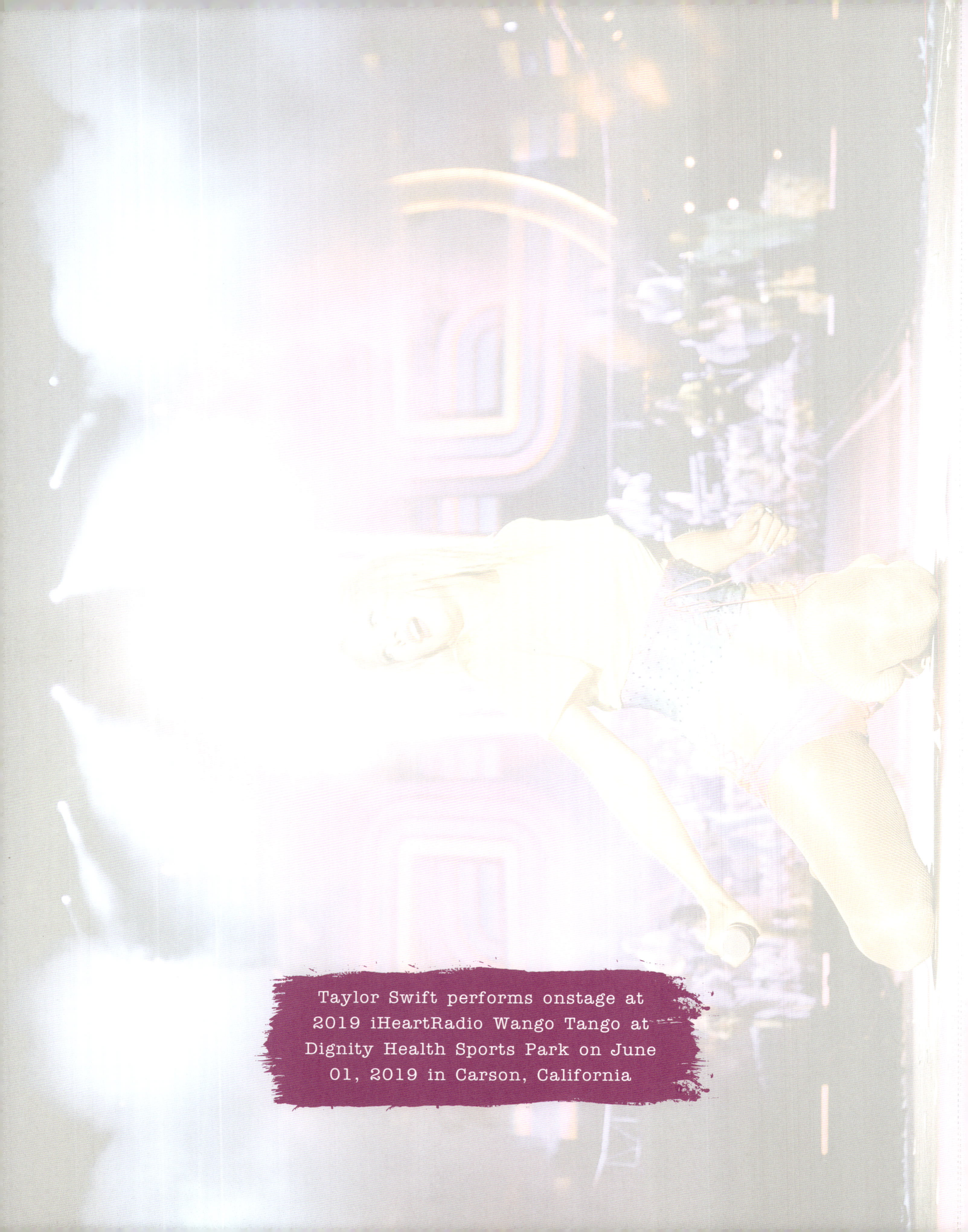

Taylor Swift performs onstage at 2019 iHeartRadio Wango Tango at Dignity Health Sports Park on June 01, 2019 in Carson, California

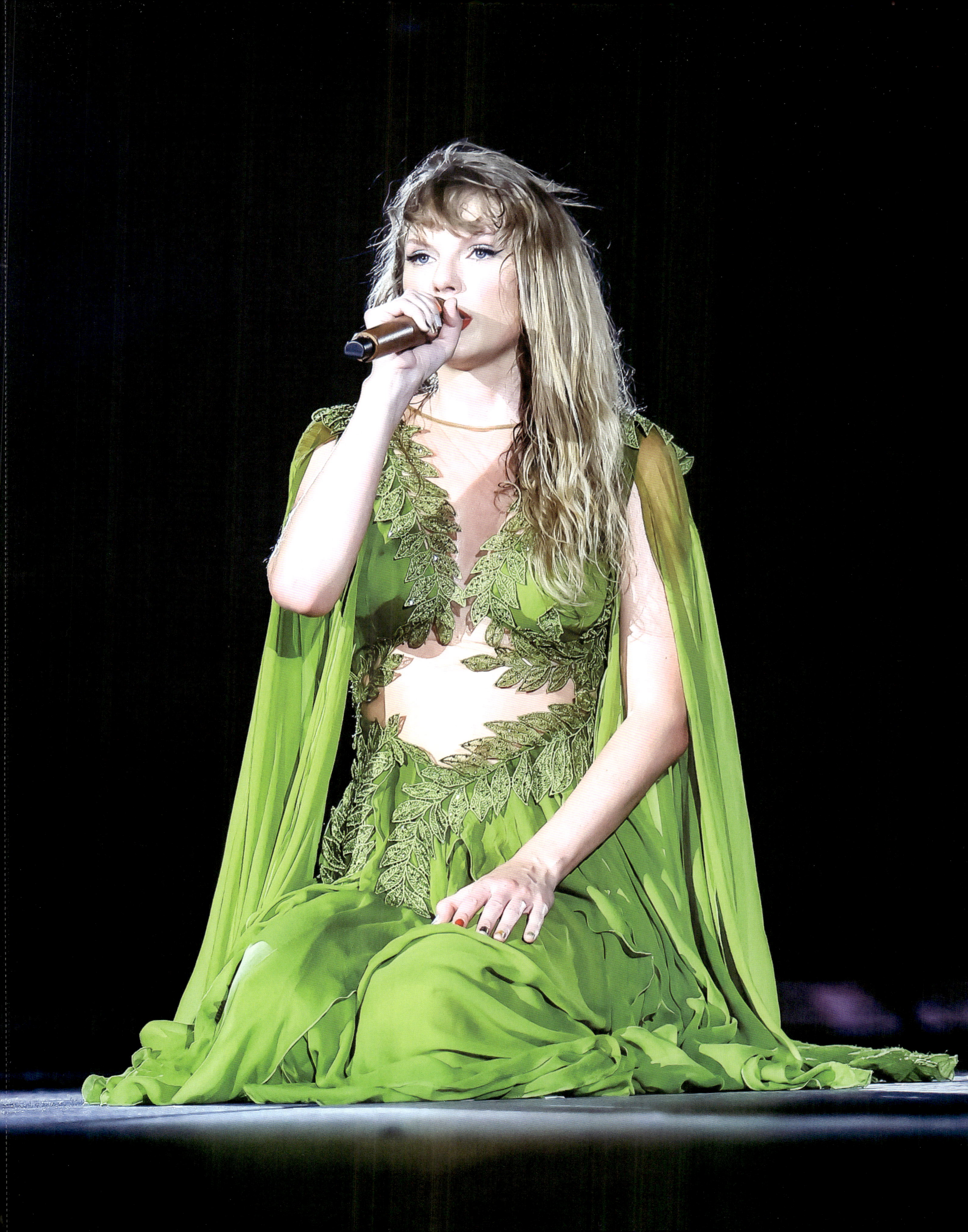

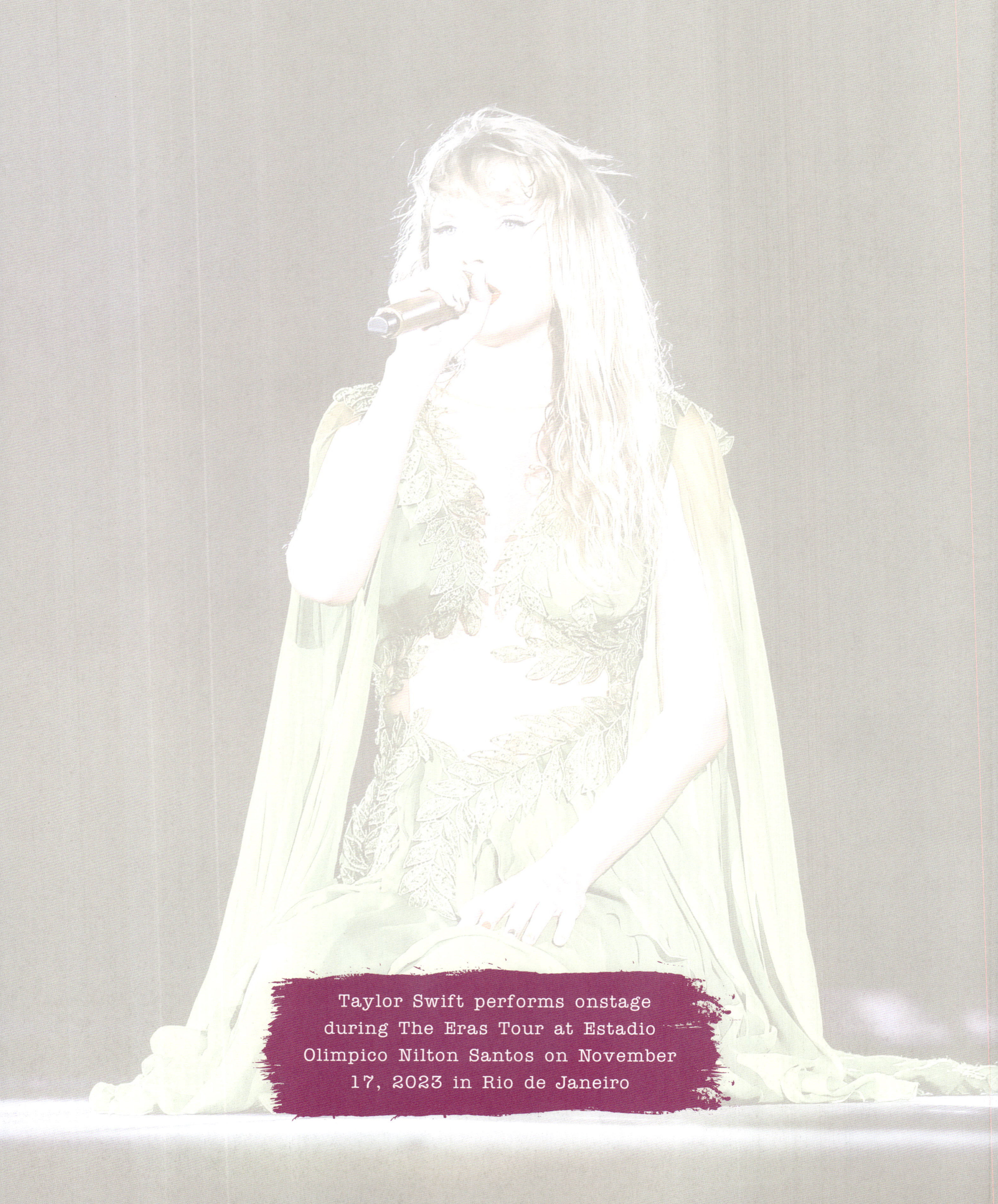

Taylor Swift performs onstage during The Eras Tour at Estadio Olimpico Nilton Santos on November 17, 2023 in Rio de Janeiro